CANADIAN Geographic

CANADA
FOR KIDS

CANADIAN Geographic

CANADA
FOR KIDS 1000 AWESOME FACTS

Aaron Kylie

FIREFLY BOOKS

A FIREFLY BOOK

Published by Firefly Books Ltd. 2020

First printing

Library of Congress Control Number: 2020938300

Library and Archives Canada Cataloguing in Publication
Title: Canadian geographic Canada for kids :
   1000 awesome facts / Aaron Kylie.
Other titles: Canada for kids |
   Canada for kids : 1000 awesome facts
Names: Kylie, Aaron, author.
Description: 2nd edition. | Previously published under title: Canada
   for kids. | Includes index.
Identifiers: Canadiana 20200247433 |
   ISBN 9780228102700 (softcover)
Subjects: LCSH: Canada—Miscellanea—Juvenile literature. |
   LCSH: Canada—Juvenile literature. |
   LCGFT: Trivia and miscellanea.
Classification: LCC FC58 .K95 2020 | DDC j971—dc23

Published in the United States by
Firefly Books (U.S.) Inc.
P.O. Box 1338, Ellicott Station
Buffalo, New York 14205

Published in Canada by
Firefly Books Ltd.
50 Staples Avenue, Unit 1
Richmond Hill, Ontario L4B 0A7

Printed in Canada

Canada ᴵ✚ᴵ

We acknowledge the financial support
of the Government of Canada.

CONTENTS

page 9

page 43

page 48

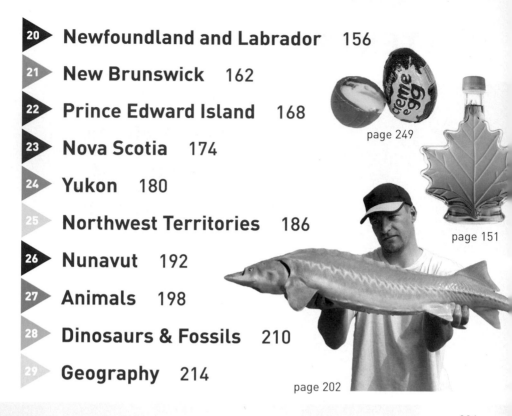

page 249

page 151

page 202

page 206

page 126

page 174

Tallest Stuff

Scraping the sky

Canada's tallest buildings

	Name	Location	Storeys/ Height (m)		Year opened
1.	First Canadian Place	Toronto	72	298	1975
2.	The St. Regis Toronto	Toronto	57	276	2012
3.	Scotia Plaza	Toronto	68	275	1988
4.	Aura	Toronto	78	272	2014
5.	TD Canada Trust Tower	Toronto	53	260	1990
6.	One Bloor	Toronto	75	257	2015
7.	Stantec	Edmonton	66	251	2018
8.	Brookfield Place East	Calgary	56	247	2017
9.	Commerce Court West	Toronto	57	239	1973
10.	The Bow	Calgary	57	237	2012

Tallest tower

It's since been eclipsed, but for 34 years (1976–2010) Toronto's CN Tower put the country on the world map as home to the globe's tallest tower, building and freestanding structure. Though it now ranks third tallest, at a mere 553.33 m, it's still no less impressive. Approximately 1.5 million people visit the tower each year to experience attractions that include a lookout, a glass floor, a revolving restaurant and the EdgeWalk (the world's highest, hands-free walk on a 1.5 m ledge encircling the building, 365 m up).

Tallest tree

You could call it the green giant. Canada's tallest recorded tree stands 56 m high. The western red cedar, located in British Columbia's Pacific Rim National Park, was discovered in 1988 and has been nicknamed "Cheewhat Giant" because of its proximity to Cheewhat Lake. The diameter of the tree is more than 6 m and contains an estimated 450 cubic m in timber volume.

Tallest timber trestle bridge

The Kinsol Trestle near the village of Shawnigan on Vancouver Island is the country's tallest timber trestle. It is also one of the largest timber bridges in the world and the highest timber trestle remaining in the Commonwealth. The 44 m high, 188 m long bridge crosses the Koksilah River. It was built in 1920.

Tallest building

At 72 storeys and 298 m high, Toronto's First Canadian Place is the country's tallest building (not tower, please note). The 2.6 million m² skyscraper was considered ahead of its time when it opened in 1975, and extensive interior and exterior rejuvenation was completed in October 2012. With the highest rooftop in Canada, it also serves as a prime communications site, second only to the nearby CN Tower.

▶ Longest Stuff

Longest coastline

If long walks on the beach are your thing, Canada's the place to be. The country's 243,000 km of coastline are the longest in the world. At a pace of about 20 km each day, the stroll would take 33 years. The shores of 52,455 islands are a big part of what makes the coastline so long.

Longest freshwater coast

Lake Huron, including Georgian Bay, has the longest freshwater coast of any lake in the world. It boasts 6,157 km of shoreline.

Longest cliff face

It really is a picture that speaks louder than words. It's difficult to describe the impressive sight of Mount Thor, a peak in Nunavut's Auyuittuq National Park. It has the world's longest uninterrupted cliff face, measuring approximately 1 km. The mountain, named after the Norse god of thunder, soars 1,675 m above sea level.

Longest freshwater beach

That's a whole lotta sand! Ontario's Wasaga Beach is the longest freshwater beach in the world. It stretches 14 km along the shore of Lake Huron's Georgian Bay.

▶▶ *Longest Stuff*

Longest golf hole

Fore! Actually, perhaps that's not necessary on Canada's longest golf hole. The 11th hole at the Nursery Golf and Country Club near Lacombe, Alberta, is a whopping 782 yards! The course's hole description notes: "Your first two shots are critical..." Indeed.

Longest paddling race

The Yukon 1000 is the world's longest paddling race. Paddlers are given 10 days to complete the 1,000 km journey, which starts in Whitehorse and ends at the Dalton highway bridge in Alaska.

Longest recreational trail

The Trans Canada Trail is the world's longest recreational trail. It is a 24,000 km network of trails that runs across the country from the Atlantic Ocean to the Pacific Ocean, connecting hundreds of communities in between. The trail, completed in 2017, extends through every Canadian province and territory.

Longest urban bike trail

Ring, ring! Looking for a long bike ride? Head to Calgary, home of the longest network of urban bike pathways on the continent and one of the largest across the globe. The city boasts some 138 km of bike-riding routes, which of course can also be used by walkers, runners and rollerbladers, too. The city even provides snow-clearing services to nearly half the system, so it can be used throughout the year.

Longest luge

The Skyline Calgary luge track is Canada's longest (and the world's second longest), at 1.8 km. The warm-weather track, which uses wheeled sleds, drops more than 100 m over its entire length. Located at the city's Winsport Olympic Park, the summer track runs along the luge course built for the 1988 Winter Games.

SLOW DOWN

▶▶ *Longest Stuff*

Longest covered bridge

The longest covered bridge on Earth is the Hartland Covered Bridge in Hartland, New Brunswick. The 391 m bridge was built in 1897 and was covered in 1921–22. Its covering was controversial, as covered bridges were known as "kissing bridges."

Longest runway

Opened in June 2014, the fourth runway at Calgary International Airport is Canada's longest, at 4,267 m long and 61 m wide. It was planned as part of the airport's $2 billion development program, in response to passenger volume doubling in the last two decades. The new landing strip is capable of landing the world's largest aircraft, the A380 and B747-800.

Longest snake

No matter what you call it, this is one long snake. And the longest native snake you'll find in Canada. Once known as the black ratsnake, but today called the gray ratsnake, the species is known to grow to 1.5 m and even longer. It is an excellent climber and is sometimes found in the cavities of hollow trees. It is typically found in southwestern Ontario, north of Lake Erie, and in the Rideau Lakes area from Kingston to Smiths Falls.

Longest swinging bridge

Looking for a swinging good time? Try the Souris Swinging Bridge in Souris, Manitoba, the nation's longest historical suspension bridge. Open to pedestrian traffic, the 177.4 m bridge was originally built in 1904. The bridge was lost in 1976 when it was taken out by water and ice, but was rebuilt and has been commemorated on a Canada Post stamp.

Longest fruit snack

In 2011, the Sun-Rype company in Kelowna, British Columbia, created a 91.44 m fruit snack that was measured by the Guinness World Records crew along a length of a football field at the Parkinson Recreation Centre. The strawberry-flavoured snack weighed 14 kg and fed hundreds of kids.

3 ▶ *Biggest Stuff*

Biggest airport

Toronto's Pearson International Airport is Canada's largest and busiest airport, and as a result, the country's primary air hub. It handles more than 30 percent of the nation's air travel. In 2018, it saw 473,000 flights and nearly 50 million passengers pass through. Pearson is the second-busiest gateway to Europe and handles the most United States–Canada air traffic.

Biggest uranium producer

Canada is the globe's largest producer of uranium, accounting for 18 percent of the world's production of the element. (Uranium is processed to create fuel for nuclear reactors.) Pictured here is the McArthur River Uranium Mine in Saskatchewan.

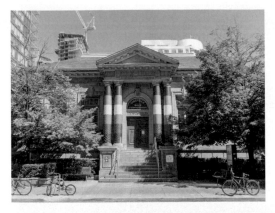

Biggest library system

The Toronto Public Library is the largest public library system in Canada. In 1998, after seven library boards of Metropolitan Toronto merged, it was the largest library system in North America at that time, serving 2.3 million. It is still one of the world's busiest library systems, with more than 17 million people visiting its 98 branches and over 29 million visiting the library's website in 2018.

Biggest salt mine

Need salt for that? Then head to Goderich, Ontario, home of the world's largest salt mine. Owned by Sifto Canada, 6,577,089 tonnes of salt are mined from the site every year.

Biggest botanical garden

The Royal Botanical Gardens in Burlington, Ontario, is the largest botanical garden in Canada, with 1,100 ha of gardens and nature reserves and more than 27 km of trails.

Biggest science lesson

Canada hosted the world's largest practical science lesson on October 12, 2012, organized by the federal government. The lesson, held at 1 p.m. EST at 88 locations across the country, focused on two experiments demonstrating Bernoulli's Principle on air pressure and included 13,701 students.

Biggest towed object

The Hibernia oil platform, located in the waters of the Grand Banks off Newfoundland, is believed to be the largest object ever towed. It took 13 days — from May 23 to June 5, 1997 — to tow the 1.08 million tonne structure from Bull Arm, Newfoundland, to the Grand Banks.

▶▶ Biggest Stuff

Biggest muscles
The bulging biceps you see here belong to none other than the undisputed king of Canadian strongmen, Jean-François Caron. "JF," as he's known on the strongman circuit, has been crowned the strongest man in Canada a whopping eight years straight from 2011 to 2018, and in 2019 he finished as the fifth-strongest man in the world at the prestigious World's Strongest Man competition. So, how strong is JF? Well, he's said to have been the seventh human known to deadlift more than 454 kg (1,000 lbs)!

►► *Biggest Stuff*

Biggest arch-and-buttress dam

Quebec's Daniel-Johnson Dam, located on the Manicouagan River some 200 km north of Baie-Comeau, is the world's largest multiple arch-and-buttress dam. The 214 m high dam, which was completed in 1968, boasts 14 buttresses across its 1,310 m length.

Biggest hydroelectric development

Let there be light! Canada's first hydroelectric power generating station was developed in 1885 to light up the city of Quebec. Today, the nation's biggest hydroelectric power development is still in Quebec — the James Bay Project. It started producing electricity in 1982. Its eight dams and 198 dikes contain five reservoirs covering 11,900 km² — half the size of Lake Ontario. The combined output of its generating stations is 10,283 megawatts.

Biggest hotel

Toronto's Eaton Chelsea is the country's largest hotel. It boasts 1,590 guestrooms and more than 2,200 m² of meeting and event space, including two ballrooms. The hotel also has four dining options.

Biggest cemetery

Montreal's Notre-Dame-des-Neiges Cemetery is the largest in Canada and the third largest on the continent. The Catholic cemetery was founded in 1854 and has more than 65,000 monuments and 71 family vaults. More than 175,000 people visit the cemetery annually.

Biggest farmers' market

With a population of only about 2,000, it's hard to believe that St. Jacobs, Ontario, located west of Toronto, is the home of the nation's largest year-round farmers' market. Approximately 4,000 Old Order Mennonites from the surrounding area are key to the market's size and success. Open Thursdays and Saturdays, the market has hundreds of vendors.

Biggest mosque

Baitun Nur Mosque in Calgary is the largest mosque complex in the country at 4,460 m². Opened on July 5, 2008, "the house of divine light" cost $15 million to build and was under construction for two years. On Fridays the mosque has more than 1,600 worshipers in attendance.

Biggest church

Canada's biggest church is in Montreal — Saint Joseph's Oratory of Mount Royal. The Roman Catholic minor basilica on Westmount Summit opened in 1967 and can seat 10,000 people. More than two million visitors and pilgrims visit the church each year.

▶▶ *Biggest Stuff*

Biggest ice cream sundae

There's plenty of ice cream to go around in Edmonton, Alberta, where the largest ice cream sundae was made. Palm Dairies Ltd made the record-breaking 54,914 lb treat in 1988.

Biggest planned explosion

Ripple Rock mountain was a killer. More than 20 large ships and at least 100 smaller vessels were sunk or damaged by the under-water mountain in the Seymour Narrows near Campbell River, British Columbia, and 114 people lost their lives as a result. So on April 5, 1958, Ripple Rock became the site of the world's largest peace time non-atomic explosion, when it was blown up to prevent further accidents.

Big dump truck

In Sparwood, British Columbia, they call it simply "the Truck." The truck in question, a 1974 Terex Titan, was the largest dump truck in the world. The 350-tonne, 20 m-long, 3,300 hp vehicle is so big, it can fit two Greyhound buses and two pickups in the box at the same time. It was decommissioned in 1991 and is now a tourist attraction.

Biggest creative output

Ontario is the country's hotbed of creativity, at least when it comes to its entertainment and publishing industries, which are the largest in Canada and the third largest in North America (after California and New York). Ontario leads the nation in film and television production, book and magazine publishing and sound recording.

Biggest museum

The Canadian Museum of History, formerly the Canadian Museum of Civilization, in Gatineau, Quebec, is the nation's largest museum. The museum boasts about five million artifacts in its collection, which attracts more than 1.2 million visitors each year.

Biggest parking lot

Looking for a parking spot? At West Edmonton Mall, that shouldn't be a problem. The mall boasts the planet's largest parking lot, with a capacity for 20,000 vehicles. A lot adjacent to the mall has space for another 10,000 cars.

Biggest zoo

The Toronto Zoo is the largest zoo in Canada. Opened on August 15, 1974, today the 284 ha facility is home to over 5,000 animals of 495 species. It attracts about 1.3 million visitors annually.

Biggest gift

The Art Gallery of Ontario's Thomson Collection, some 2,000 works of Canadian and European art collected by Canadian businessman Ken Thomson, is the largest gift ever made to a Canadian cultural institution.

▶ *Smallest Stuff*

Smallest mammal

They weigh just 12.4 grams, so it's little wonder that the pygmy shrew is the smallest mammal in the Americas. Often described as something between a mouse and a mole, these shrews are small: their head and body average length is about 5.1 to 6.4 cm. They can be found throughout most of eastern Canada.

Smallest bird

Keep your eyes peeled: Canada's smallest bird is the calliope hummingbird, which is about 7 cm long (shown life size here) and weighs just 2.5 grams. It's found in central British Columbia and southwestern Alberta.

Tiny house

It's hard to say what record, if any, the tiny house at 128 Day Avenue in Toronto holds, but there's no doubt it's one small house. Measuring 2.2 m wide and 14.3 m long, the home was built in 1912. It's still lived in today.

Smallest jail

Hope you're not a claustrophobic crook. The Rodney Jail, in Rodney, Ontario, bills itself as the smallest jail in North America. Built in 1890, the jail is 4.57 m by 5.49 m.

Smallest desert

When you think of Canada, and when you think of the North, you naturally think of deserts — or maybe not! But Canada is home to what's called the world's smallest desert, the Carcross Desert in Yukon. The area's dry climate and strong winds have created a small 260-ha series of sand dunes — but it's not technically a desert.

CARCROSS DESERT

Oldest Stuff

Oldest mine

The oldest operating mine in Canada is the Copper Cliff North Mine near Sudbury, Ontario, which began operation in 1886.

Oldest water

With all the water in Canada, is it any wonder that the oldest known water on the planet was found in Ontario? University of Toronto geoscientist Barbara Sherwood Lollar and her colleagues discovered the 2.6-billion-year-old water some 2.4 km below the earth in a mine near Timmins, Ontario.

Oldest maple tree

Canada's known for many things, and a big one is maple syrup. The oldest known sugar maple tree in the country is estimated to be at least 500 years old, and it's found in southwestern Ontario's North Pelham area. The Comfort Maple, as it's known, stands about 30.5 m tall and has a trunk circumference of 6 m.

Oldest wooden house

There's a special house at 477 St. George Street in Annapolis Royal, Nova Scotia. The privately owned house, a provincially and municipally designated heritage building, is the oldest wooden house in Canada. The original house was built in 1693 but was burned in 1707, only to be rebuilt in 1708 on the original foundation.

Oldest university building

The oldest university building in Canada still being used as part of a university campus is Sir Howard Douglas Hall (Old Arts Building) at the University of New Brunswick. The building officially opened on January 1, 1829.

Oldest canal system

The Rideau Canal, which runs from the Ottawa River to Lake Ontario and the St. Lawrence River at Kingston, is the oldest continuously operated canal system in North America. Opened in 1832, the Rideau is 202 km long and boasts 47 locks that connect lakes and rivers through the region. It is a national historic site and a UNESCO world heritage site.

Oldest English university

The oldest public English-language university in Canada — and one of the oldest universities in North America — is the University of New Brunswick. Its Fredericton campus was established in 1785 (the Saint John campus was created in 1964).

Oldest French university

The Université Laval in Quebec City is the oldest French-language university in North America. Established in 1663, today the school has nearly 50,000 students and more than 270,000 graduates.

Oldest courthouse

There's been a lot of order in this court. The Argyle Township Court House & Gaol, in Tusket, Nova Scotia, is the country's oldest standing courthouse. Built in 1805, it operated until 1944 — the jail closed in 1924 followed by the courthouse 20 years later.

▶▶ *Oldest Stuff*

Oldest part of North America

The Canadian Shield, which is about
4.4 million km² in size, covers about half of
Canada — and encircles Hudson Bay — was
the first part of North America permanently
above sea level. It is also the oldest section
of the continent's crustal plate (a layer of
the Earth's surface) and the largest area of
exposed Precambrian rock (formed about
500 million years ago) on the planet.

Oldest and longest footpath

The Bruce Trail, which runs from Niagara to Tobermory in Ontario along the Niagara Escarpment, is the nation's oldest and longest marked footpath. The trail stretches for 890 km, with another 400 km of associated trails. Pictured here is a portion of the trail around Georgian Bay.

Oldest military school

Today, all cadets at the Royal Military College of Canada in Kingston, Ontario, know the names of "the Old Eighteen," the school's first class of students in 1874. The RMC is the nation's oldest military school, which was founded to train Canadian cadets in all aspects of the military profession.

Oldest co-ed boarding school

Albert College in Belleville, Ontario, is Canada's oldest co-educational boarding and day school. Established in 1857, the school educates students from pre-kindergarten to grade 12, and students in grade 7 and up can live on campus.

Oldest student publication

Toronto's Upper Canada College private school is home to the nation's oldest continuously running student publication. The *College Times* has been published since 1871.

▶▶ *Oldest Stuff*

Oldest ferry

Halifax is home to the continent's oldest, continuously running saltwater ferry service, which began in 1752. Known as "the Dartmouth ferry" at the time, the service connected the vast farmland on the Dartmouth side of Halifax Harbour with Halifax, providing the city with fresh food. The original ferry was a rowboat with a sail.

Oldest sternwheeler

The SS *Moyie* is the world's oldest intact passenger sternwheeler. The ship was retired in 1957 after 59 years of service for the Canadian Pacific Railway's BC Lake and River Service. The *Moyie* performed a number of duties over its lifetime and was the last operating sternwheeler in Canada. The ship is a national historic site today at its home in Kaslo, British Columbia.

Oldest rocks

The oldest known rocks on Earth — 250 million years older than any other known rocks — are found in Canada. Geologists discovered the 4.28-billion-year-old rock in 2001 in an area of exposed bedrock on the eastern shore of Hudson Bay, in northern Quebec.

Oldest Canadian club outside of Canada

The Canada Club in London, England, founded in 1810, is the oldest Canadian club outside of Canada. Originally formed by fur traders of the North West Company, today the club is open to all with an interest in Canada. It hosts two dinners a year featuring keynote speakers of significance to Canadians. Every Canadian prime minister has addressed the club.

▶▶ *Oldest Stuff*

Oldest candy company

If you're a Canadian candy connoisseur, you'll appreciate this. Ganong Bros. Limited of St. Stephen, New Brunswick, is Canada's oldest candy company. It was established in 1873. The business is responsible for a number of candy firsts: the first Canadian lollipop in 1895; the first chocolate nut bar in North America in 1910; the first heart-shaped box for chocolates (introduced originally for Christmas) in 1932; and the first fruit snack made from real fruit in purée form in 1988.

Oldest marathon

When it comes to legendary road running races, one thinks of Boston and New York. But Hamilton, Ontario? One should, as it's home to the oldest marathon in North America (preceding Boston's by three years), the Around the Bay Road Race, which was first run in 1894. The 30 km race has been won by the best in the world, including Olympic medallists and Boston Marathon winners.

Oldest sporting event

Here's betting you didn't know that the Royal St. John's Regatta is the oldest sporting event in North America. It's also known as "the largest garden party in the world," thanks to the socializing that accompanies the rowing races. The first record of the event is from 1818; however, crews were known to compete in the St. John's Harbour since the 1700s. Today, the event, held annually in August, draws 50,000 spectators to the shores of Quidi Vidi Lake.

Oldest golf club

The Royal Montreal Golf Club is the oldest golf club in North America. Formed as the Montreal Golf Club in 1873 (it received the Royal designation in 1884), the first course was nine holes on Fletcher's Field, part of Mount Royal Park on the outskirts of Montreal.

Oldest French community

Tadoussac, Quebec, is well known as a launching point for great whale watching in the St. Lawrence River. It's also the oldest continuously inhabited French community in America. Known as the cradle of New France, Tadoussac was first settled in 1600.

Oldest company

The Hudson's Bay Company, founded in 1670, is North America's oldest continuously operating company. In its earliest days, the business was instrumental in European development in the country, particularly its eastern half, where numerous outposts were set up to trade goods. Today, HBC runs the country's largest department store, with 90 locations across the nation.

Oldest horse race

The Queen's Plate, held annually since 1860, is the oldest continuously run horse race in North America. Today, it's run each July at Toronto's Woodbine Racetrack. The race has been attended by reigning monarchs five times in its history, and by representatives of the monarchy another dozen times.

6 ▶ Fastest Stuff

World's fastest human (muscle-powered vehicle) and Canada's fastest cyclist

In 2015, Saskatchewan native Todd Reichert claimed the title of fastest bicyclist on Earth from the World Human-Powered Vehicle Association when he pedalled a bicycle at 139.44 km per hour in Battle Mountain, Nevada, making Reichert the world's fastest human (using a completely muscle-powered vehicle). In 2016, he shattered his own record with a stunning 144.17 kmph run in the 200 m flying start speed trial.

Canada's second-fastest cyclist

Up until 2013, Sam Whittingham, native of Quadra Island, British Columbia, was considered the fastest bicyclist in the world. He earned the title on September 18, 2009, at Battle Mountain, Nevada, when he clocked 133.28 km per hour in the men's 200 m flying start. He still holds three cycling speed records from the World Human-Powered Vehicle Association.

Fastest ghost-pepper eater

Mike Jack of London, Ontario, is the world-record holder in speed eating ghost peppers. In 2019, Guinness World Records clocked him eating three peppers in 9.75 seconds and he also ate the most peppers in one minute (97 grams). In 2020 he ate the largest volume of the peppers in a timed sitting (246 grams), which was 100 grams more than the previous record holder. And, just for the record, a ghost pepper (also known as a Bhut Jolokia pepper) is 2,314 times as hot as Frank's Red Hot sauce. Yikes!

Fastest bird

You do NOT want to be the prey of the peregrine falcon. Why? When hunting, peregrines can dive at more than 300 km per hour, making them the fastest bird in the world. The highest recorded speed of a peregrine is reported to be 389 km per hour. Peregrines can be found in Canada and other places across the globe, except for New Zealand, Antarctica and Iceland.

Fastest ice

It's hardly surprising that the so-called "fastest ice in the world" is in Canada. Specifically, it's at the Olympic Oval in Calgary, built for the 1988 Winter Olympic Games. It's earned the honour thanks to the 258 long track and 30 short track world records set on the surface. Why so quick? The ice is made with demineralized water, which reduces the amount of dirt and mineral buildup that can create friction between ice and skate. Less friction equals faster ice. The track was also the first fully covered 400 m oval in North America.

Fastest animal

The pronghorn antelope, found in southern Alberta and Saskatchewan, is the fastest land animal in North America, capable of reaching speeds up to 72 km per hour in short bursts and sustaining speeds up to 60 km per hour over longer distances. Its speeds over longer distances lead some to consider it the fastest land animal in the world.

▶▶ *Fastest Stuff*

 Most soccer ball touches, 60 and 30 seconds
According to Guinness World Records, Canadian Chloe Hegland holds the record for most touches of a soccer ball (while keeping it in the air) in one minute by a female — 339. She set the record on November 3, 2007, while filming a Guinness special in Beijing, China. Hegland also holds the record for most touches of a soccer ball (while keeping it in the air) in 30 seconds by a female (163), according to Guinness World Records. Hegland achieved the feat on February 23, 2008.

 **Fastest bike relay across Canada**
The fastest cycling relay across Canada, according to Guinness World Records, is 8 days, 8 hours and 14 minutes. A team of five Canadians — Matt Young, Kyle Bagnano, Willie Cormack, Richard Alm and Keith Nicoll — set the record between September 14 and 22, 2007, cycling from Halifax to Vancouver. Their average speed? Forty km per hour.

 Fastest bike ride across Canada
Here's a long, fast bike ride. According to Guinness World Records, the fastest time to cycle across Canada is 13 days, 6 hours and 13 minutes. Canadian Arvid Loewen set the mark between July 1 and 14, 2011, travelling 6,037 km from Vancouver to Halifax.

Fastest half-marathon (siblings)

They say a family that runs together breaks records together. Well, this theory seemed to work for siblings Valentina and Andrea Caballero of Mississauga, Ontario, who, on October 20, 2019, managed to set a new world record for fastest half-marathon by a pair of siblings. The sisters crossed the finish line of the Scotia-bank Toronto Waterfront Half Marathon together in record time — 2:15:49, breaking the previous record of 2:30:00.

Fastest run across Canada

The fastest trip across Canada on foot by a man (Al Howie of England), took 72 days, 10 hours and 23 minutes, according to Guinness World Records. The 7,295.5 km trek from St. John's to Victoria took place from June 21 to September 1, 1991. The fastest trip across Canada on foot by a woman (Canadian Ann Keane), took 143 days. According to Guinness World Records, Keane travelled 7,831 km from St. John's to Tofino, British Columbia, between April 17 and September 8, 2002.

Record-Setting Stuff

Heavy over 100

Kevin Fast (see Aircraft pulling) also holds the record for the heaviest vehicle pulled over 100 feet, according to Guinness World Records. On July 5, 2017, Fast pulled a 90,060 kg vehicle more than 30.48 m over level ground.

Longest beard

Sarwan Singh of Surrey, British Columbia, has the longest beard in the world according to Guinness World Records. Singh's beard, measured on March 4, 2010, was 2.495 m long.

Juggling chainsaws

Ian Stewart of Turo, Nova Scotia, achieved the most chainsaw juggling catches ever (105), according to Guinness World Records. Stewart set the record on September 6, 2019.

World-record singer

Singer/songwriter Justin Bieber added this accomplishment to his list of achievements in 2015; he holds the Guinness World Record title as the youngest male solo artist to debut at No. 1 on the Billboard Hot 100. He was 21 years and 202 days old when his single "What Do You Mean?" topped the charts.

Largest human maple leaf

In June 2019, close to 4,000 Trenton, Ontario, community members donned red shirts and came together to form the largest human maple leaf. The community set out to support "Soldier On," an initiative that helps active military members and veterans who are injured or are dealing with mental health issues. The group broke the previous Guinness World Record set by a town in Grouse Mountain, British Columbia.

Largest Dairy Queen ice cream cake

On May 10, 2011, the Dairy Queen at Yonge and Dundas in Toronto, Ontario, made it into the Guinness World Records with the largest ice cream cake ever made. The cake weighed 10.13 tonnes and was 14 ft 7 in long, 13 ft 3 in wide, and 3 ft 3 in tall.

Largest actual maple leaf

Here's another record with a special Canadian connection. The largest recorded maple leaf (actual leaf!) was found on December 14, 2010, in Richmond, British Columbia, by Vikas Tanwar and family. The leaf — 53 cm wide, 52.2 cm tall, with a 32.5 cm stem — was confirmed as the biggest ever found by Guinness World Records.

Aircraft pulling

Kevin Fast of Cobourg, Ontario, holds the distinction of the heaviest aircraft pull in the world, according to Guinness World Records. Fast pulled a CC-173 Globemaster III, weighing 188.83 tonnes, 8.8 m at Canadian Forces Base Trenton, in Trenton, Ontario, on September 17, 2009.

Notable Firsts

First to swim across Lake Ontario

You could call it the first great lake swim. Marilyn Bell, born in Toronto on November 19, 1937, was the first person to swim across Lake Ontario. At just 16 years old, Bell completed the swim from Youngstown, New York, to Toronto on September 9, 1954. It took her 20 hours and 59 minutes to swim the estimated 51.5 km course.

Youngest to swim the English Channel

Marilyn Bell was the youngest person to swim the English Channel. She achieved that feat (which has since been eclipsed) on July 31, 1955, at the age of 17.

Youngest to swim Juan de Fuca Strait

One more long-distance swimming mark for Marilyn Bell: on August 23, 1956, Bell became the youngest person to swim across British Columbia's Juan de Fuca Strait. She completed the crossing in 10 hours and 39 minutes, after which she retired from marathon swimming. In 2017, 52-year-old Susan Simmons swam the straight in a record time of 10 hours and six minutes.

First to swim the English Channel both ways

There must be something in the water near Toronto. Cindy Nicholas, born on August 20, 1957, in Ontario's capital, was the first woman to swim the English Channel both ways non-stop. She accomplished the record swim on September 8, 1977, in 19 hours and 55 minutes.

First Canadian spacewoman

On January 22, 1992, Dr. Roberta Bondar, a native of Sault Ste. Marie, Ontario, became the first Canadian woman in space and the second Canadian to leave the planet. During her eight-day mission on the space shuttle *Discovery*, Bondar conducted experiments to help find ways to allow future astronauts to take prolonged flights.

Youngest skier to South Pole

In 2004, when she was 18, Iqaluit native Sarah McNair-Landry became the youngest person in the world to ski to the South Pole. The more than 1,100 km trek, which she did with her brother, took her 52 days to complete.

First Canadian spaceman

Quebec City native Marc Garneau became the first Canadian to fly in space on October 5, 1984. Garneau was a payload specialist on NASA shuttle mission 41-G. He returned to space in 1996 and 2000, and in total logged more than 677 hours in space.

▶▶ *Notable Firsts*

First female doctor

The first Canadian woman to practise medicine in Canada was Emily Stowe (right) of Norwich, Ontario, who started working as a doctor in Toronto in 1867. Her daughter, Augusta Stowe Gullen, was the first woman to earn a medical degree in Canada. She studied at the Toronto School of Medicine and graduated from Victoria College in Cobourg, Ontario, in 1883.

First licensed female doctor

In 1875, Jennie Trout of Stratford, Ontario, became the first woman in Canada licensed to practise medicine. Trout was encouraged in the endeavour by Emily Stowe (left). Trout practised at Toronto's Therapeutic and Electrical Institute until 1882.

First Canadian space commander

Astronaut Chris Hadfield became the first Canadian to command a spaceship on March 13, 2013. Hadfield was commander of the International Space Station during the second part of his five-month stay there. Hadfield's mission ended on May 13, 2013, after 146 days in space (144 on the ISS). He travelled nearly 99.8 million km during his mission.

Youngest super-nova spotter

Nathan Gray of Greenwood, Nova Scotia, spotted supernova SN 2013hc in the constellation of Draco on October 30, 2013, when he was only 10 years old! His discovery bested the previous record holder, his sister Kathryn, by just 33 days.

First Canadian to win Boston Marathon

Tom Longboat, born on July 4, 1887, in Six Nations, Ontario, was the first Canadian to win the Boston Marathon, the world's oldest annual marathon (it was first run in 1897). Longboat won the legendary race in 1907.

First Canadian to climb Everest

Talk about the height of sports. Laurie Skreslet, born in Calgary on October 25, 1949, was the first Canadian to climb to the summit of Mount Everest, the world's tallest peak. He did it just before his 33rd birthday, October 5, 1982.

First Canadian woman to climb Everest

Another Canadian also set a significant milestone on Everest. Sharon Wood, born in Halifax on May 18, 1957, was the first woman from the western hemisphere to reach the summit of Mount Everest. She completed the climb on May 20, 1986.

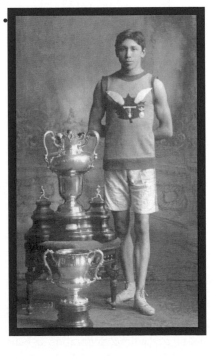

►► *Notable Firsts*

First polar dives

You could call him Canada's very own coldwater man. Dr. Joseph MacInnis, born in Barrie, Ontario, on March 2, 1937, led the teams that made the first scientific dives at the North Pole in the 1970s.

First polar undersea station

Dr. Joseph MacInnis also built the world's first polar undersea station. Dubbed the Sub-Igloo, the capsule had room for four and was established under the ice in the Northwest Passage in 1972.

Deepest dive

Now here's a story with depth. James Cameron, born in Kapuskasing, Ontario, and the director of the Oscar-winning films *Titanic* and *Avatar*, became the first person to dive solo to the deepest part of the world's oceans. On March, 26, 2012, Cameron visited the Mariana Trench in the Pacific Ocean, some 11 km below the surface, in a custom-built submarine, *Deepsea Challenger*.

First quints

They brought a whole new meaning to the phrase "Take five." The Dionne quintuplets, born in Corbeil, Ontario, on May 28, 1934, were the first quintuplets in the world to survive more than a few days. They would become the biggest tourist attraction in the nation at the time, generating an estimated $500 million for the province of Ontario and attracting some three million people to see them in person. They are pictured here with their delivering doctor, Allan Roy Dafoe.

First Canadian stamp

In 1851, the first Canadian postage stamp, the Three-Pence Beaver, was designed by Sir Sandford Fleming. The design was one of the first in the world to feature a pictorial, as opposed to a portrait of a monarch, a statesman, a geometric design or a coat of arms. The first of these stamps was issued on April 23 of that year.

First photograph of Canada

What else other than Ontario's Niagara Falls would appear in the first known picture of Canada? It was taken by English industrial chemist H.L. Pattinson during a visit to America. The plate on which the image of Horseshoe Falls appears is marked April 1840 on the back. A total of eight of Pattinson's plates from this trip have been discovered, a number of which show buildings in Niagara Falls, including the Clifton Hotel, which was frequented by dignitaries of the time.

Innovations | **Food**

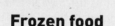

Frozen food

If you're a fan of fish sticks — or any frozen food for that matter — you can thank marine scientist Archibald Huntsman. In 1926, while working for the Biological Board of Canada (later the Fisheries Research Board) in Halifax, Huntsman began work on developing a commercial frozen fish product. The result? Ice Fillets debuted in 1929 in Toronto, marking the first time frozen food was sold to the public. The product was pricey but popular. Unfortunately, fishing companies lost interest, and Ice Fillets were abandoned in 1931.

Peanut butter

Here's something nutty: Montreal's Marcellus Gilmore Edson was the first person to patent modern peanut butter in 1884.

Pizza Pops

Paul Faraci invented this miniature version of the traditional Italian calzone or panzerotti in Winnipeg, Manitoba, in 1964.

Best potato for french fries

If you eat french fries, there's a good chance you've eaten a Canadian food innovation. The Shepody potato, released by Agri-Food Canada's research lab in Fredericton, New Brunswick, in 1983, quickly became one of the world's most popular potatoes for french fries. The Shepody is known for its short growing season and high yields.

Canada Dry ginger ale

You knew this! Canada Dry ginger ale was created in Canada, by Toronto chemist and pharmacist John J. McLaughlin. He's said to have perfected the recipe in 1904.

Sugar-free pop and pop cans

A couple more firsts for the pop industry from the makers of Canada Dry: during the 1950s and 1960s, the company was the first of the major soft drink makers to market sugar-free beverages, and the first to put pop in cans.

▶▶ *Innovations* | **Food**

Pablum

The nutritious baby food Pablum was created in 1930 by Alan Brown, Theo Drake and Fred Tisdall, to help prevent and treat rickets in children. The popular product improved the health of millions of children around the world and led to ideas for a number of other nutritious foods for infants. The three doctors at Toronto's Sick Kids Hospital donated royalties from the product back to the hospital.

Yukon Gold potatoes

The Yukon Gold potato naturally was created in Canada. Bred at the University of Guelph in 1966, the Yukon Gold is known for its longevity in storage, as well as being a very good potato for baking, boiling and french-frying. It was released to market in 1981.

Red Fife wheat

Canadian wheat is known as some of the finest in the world. The oldest of the nation's wheat varieties is Red Fife, which was first grown in Peterborough, Ontario, on the farm of Dave Fife in 1842. Red Fife was known as a fine milling and baking wheat, and by the 1860s it was being cultivated across the nation. Red Fife was considered the country's wheat standard for more than four decades, from about 1860 to 1900.

Marquis wheat

In the early 1900s, a Canadian-produced wheat called Marquis replaced Red Fife as the nation's top wheat. It was a cross between Red Fife and Hard Red Calcutta. Marquis matured seven to 10 days earlier than Red Fife and produced a great yield of 41.6 bushels per acre, while retaining the baking quality of Fife. The yield and quality of Marquis made Canada the largest wheat-exporting nation on the planet.

McIntosh apple

If apple pie is a traditional American dish, the McIntosh apple is as Canadian as it gets. In 1811, John McIntosh discovered an apple sapling on his farm near Dundela, Ontario, that subsequently produced a fruit with a great taste, texture, aroma and appearance. It was also ideally suited for growing in Canada's colder climate. John's son Allan established a nursery for the species and promoted it widely. It has since become one of the most popular apple varieties in Canada and around the world.

Spartan apples

Here's another great Canadian food invention: the Spartan apple. The variety was first developed in Summerland, British Columbia, by R.C. Palmer at a federal experimental farm. Interestingly, the exact parentage of the species is in question. It was once thought to be a cross between a McIntosh and a Newtown, but testing has ruled out the Newtown.

Green plastic garbage bag

Three Canadians lay claim to the invention of an indispensible household product: the green plastic garbage bag. Harry Wasylyk of Winnipeg, Larry Hanson at Union Carbide in Lindsay, Ontario, and Frank Plomp of Toronto all came up with variations of the polyethylene bags in the 1950s, which were originally sold to hospitals and businesses.

Paint roller

It's oh, so simple! And saves countless backbreaking hours of work. Plus, it's hardly changed in more than 80 years: the paint roller. It was invented by Norman Breakey of Toronto in 1940. Unfortunately, Breakey never got to roll in the profits, as he was never able to make enough rollers to profit from it before competitors made slightly different variations and sold it as their own invention.

Robertson screwdriver

What do you do when you screw up? Invent a new screwdriver. After cutting his hand using a springloaded screwdriver in Montreal, Peter Lymburner Robertson decided to improve the tool. The result: the Robertson Drive screwdriver, which was patented in 1909. The square-headed driver and screw could be driven more quickly and reduced the slipping common with other screwdrivers.

Jolly Jumper

The Jolly Jumper, the device designed for infants, was invented by Canadian Susan Olivia Poole in 1910. The original was made for Poole's first child, Joseph. It wasn't until 1948 — and after all seven of Poole's children had used the device — that the Jolly Jumper was mass produced for retail.

First light bulb

Thomas Edison gets all the recognition, but a Toronto medical student named Henry Woodward, with help from a city innkeeper named Matthew Evans, developed and patented a predecessor to Edison's light bulb in 1874. The duo didn't have the money to produce and sell the bulbs and sold the patent in 1875 to Edison. His light bulb debuted in 1879.

Alkaline battery

You'll get a charge out of this one. Canadian Lewis Urry invented the alkaline battery in 1959. About 80 percent of dry cell batteries in use in the world are based on Urry's invention.

Snowmobile

While there were patents for snowmobiles that pre-dated his, Joseph-Armand Bombardier is widely considered the inventor of the modern-day snowmobile. Born in Sherbrooke, Quebec, on April 16, 1907, Bombardier invented his first snowmobile in 1937, which was successful largely because of the front steering skis and the rear tracked drive. In 1959, Bombardier debuted the Ski-Doo snowmobile, the motorcycle-sized version of his original invention.

Snowplow

What else would a Canadian dentist invent but the first rotary snowplow? Huh? Indeed, Toronto's Dr. J.W. Elliott invented the machine in 1869. But one was never built until the winter of 1883–84 another Canadian, Orange Jull, improved on the original design. Designed for trains, the invention became standard on trains through the winter.

Walkie-talkie

Canadian Donald L. Hings invented the walkie-talkie in 1937. The first versions of the device were designed as portable radios for bush pilots working for Consolidated Mining and Smelting (now Teck), where Hings was employed. It wasn't until the Second World War, when the company lent Hings to the Department of National Defence and the National Research Council, that the walkie-talkie became widely used.

Artifical fur

A Canadian project during the Second World War to develop better Arctic clothing for the military led to the first patent for artificial fur.

Snow blower

This is hardly a surprise. The snow blower was invented by Canadian Arthur Sicard, born in Saint-Leonard-de-Port-Maurice, Quebec, in 1925. He sold the first commercial self-propelled rotary machine in 1927. The blower was made of a four-wheel-drive truck chassis, a truck motor, a snow blower head with two adjustable chutes and another motor to drive the snow blower head.

Cosmetics firsts

Shhh. Here's a uniquely Canadian beauty secret: Elizabeth Arden, the international cosmetics company, was founded by a Canadian. Born in Woodbridge, Ontario, on December 31, 1884, Florence Nightingale Graham (who changed her name to Elizabeth Arden) opened a beauty salon on New York City's Fifth Avenue in 1910. She is known for a number of firsts in the cosmetics industry, including creating the first travel-sized beauty products.

IMAX

IMAX, a movie format that can record and display motion pictures at a far greater size and resolution than traditional film systems, was developed by a group of Canadian filmmakers and unveiled at the Fuji Pavilion at EXPO '70 in Osaka, Japan. The first IMAX projection system debuted at Toronto's Ontario Place in 1971. The world's first IMAX 3D system was revealed at Vancouver's EXPO '86. There are now more than 1,500 IMAX theatres in 80 countries.

Trivial Pursuit

How else to address this than with a question: Where was the popular game Trivial Pursuit invented? In Montreal, when journalists Chris Haney and Scott Abbott came up with the idea on December 15, 1979.

►► *Innovations*
Space & Flight

Canadarm

Quick, name the famed Canadian invention known as the Shuttle Remote Manipulator System. The device, more commonly known as the Canadarm, debuted on the space shuttle *Columbia* on November 13, 1981. It subsequently performed 90 shuttle missions over 30 years, before being retired from NASA's shuttle program. The technological advances it inspired live on in a family of robotics developed for the International Space Station.

First black hole

Dr. Tom Bolton was the first to discover a black hole. Bolton discovered Cygnus X-1 from the David Dunlap Observatory, just north of Toronto, in 1971.

Avro Arrow

It's been called Canada's greatest aeronautical achievement. The Avro Arrow, or CF-105 jet fighter, was the only supersonic jet the country produced. It is said to have been faster (it had a maximum speed of 2,453 km per hour) and more advanced than any other comparable aircraft. Rising costs of production combined with the development of long-range missiles caused the government to cancel the aircraft (on February 20, 1959, a day known as "Black Friday" by some as a result), and all the existing jets were destroyed, along with all related plans and equipment.

Pressure suit

Wilbur Franks, born in Weston, Ontario, and a graduate of the University of Toronto, was a medical researcher who invented the pressure suit, which allows pilots to perform high-speed acrobatics without passing out. The suit was first used in 1942 by Allied fighter pilots during the Second World War. Today's space suits are considered subtle refinements of Franks' invention.

Human centrifuge

Franks was also responsible for the construction of the nation's first human centrifuge (also the first in Allied nations), which was built for the pressure-suit project in 1941. The lab in Toronto, which was used to test the suit and train jet pilots to withstand g-forces, eventually became the RCAF Institute of Aviation Medicine.

►► *Innovations*
Space & Flight

First Earth observatory satellite
The first high-resolution satellite image ever taken of the South Pole was captured in 1997 from Canada's first Earth observation satellite system, RADARSAT-1. Launched on November 4, 1995, RADARSAT-1 was capable of acquiring images of Earth in any conditions, day or night, rain or shine.

First landing pad for UFOs
Who needs Area 51? Canada has the world's first UFO landing pad. The unique landmark was built in the town of St. Paul, Alberta, and opened on June 3, 1967. In 1996, a UFO interpretive centre was built to accompany the pad.

First television satellite
Launched on January 17, 1976, Hermes, a collaborative effort between Canada and the United States, was the first satellite to broadcast television signals into homes. The most powerful satellite at the time, Hermes demonstrated direct broadcasting to Peru, Australia and Papua New Guinea, in addition to experiments conducted in Canada and the United States.

First stratospheric balloon
In September 2013, the Canadian Space Agency, in partnership with the French space agency (Centre national d'études spatiales), completed the first launch of a stratospheric research balloon in Canada. The remote-controlled balloon was launched from Timmins, Ontario. It can haul up to 1.58 tonnes of equipment, requires no fuel and is fully recoverable.

Third nation in space

Canada became the third nation in space — after the United States and the USSR — on September 29, 1962, with the launch of the research satellite Alouette-I. Designed to last for one year, the satellite ultimately performed flawlessly for 10 years.

First communications satellite

The Anik A1 was the world's first domestic geostationary communications satellite system. It was launched on November 9, 1972. The system enabled Telesat Canada to provide high-quality telephone service to Canada's north and television service across the country.

Automatic landing system

Electronics engineer Eric William Leaver, who grew up in Saskatchewan, invented an inertial guidance system (automatic landing system) for aircraft in the 1930s. Subsequent products based on his invention are used all over the world today.

Crash position indicator

The crash position indicator, an emergency beacon locator for aircraft, was invented in 1957 by the National Research Council's Harry Stevinson. It was used for the first time that year by the military to locate a downed airplane. By the 1960s, the device was in use on commercial airlines.

First concussion sensors in high school

There's no shortage of concussion talk these days in sports. And thankfully, lots of experts are doing their best to prevent head injuries. In the fall of 2013, Calgary's Ernest Manning High School became the first secondary school in Canada to install specifically designed sensors (called the Shockbox) in their helmets to measure the impact of collisions. Calgary's Canadian Football League team, the Stampeders, were the first pigskin club in the country to employ the device.

Bomb detector

While working at the National Research Council in the 1980s, chemist Lorne Elias developed a portable explosive vapour detector, a device capable of sniffing out hidden bombs. In 1984, the RCMP used a prototype of the device during a visit by the Pope. When security officials were checking the Pope's baggage, a detector went off — triggered by a revolver one of the pontiff's bodyguards had packed in his luggage.

Kid-proof phones

So you want a cell phone, but first you need to convince your parents to let you have one. Well Kytephone is your answer. This mobile app turns any Android phone or tablet into a secure space for kids of all ages. Martin Drashkov and Renat Gataullin, both based in Toronto, created the app so kids can enjoy surfing the web or playing games on their phones, while at the same time granting parents a way to monitor their kids' online activity with ease. Now that's a winning solution.

Voice mimicry

The lyrebird is an Australian terrestrial bird that mimics sounds it hears in its surrounding environment. It's only fitting that Lyrebird AI, a Montreal-based artificial intelligence company, would borrow from the ground-dwelling bird's name, as mimicry is exactly what their technology aims to do. Lyrebird AI uses the human voice and imitates it — so much so that an entire fake conversation between two or more people could potentially be created. That could give a whole new meaning to the term "fake news."

Showbie

School's in! Literally, school can be in session even at home with the help of Showbie. The Canadian-made homework drop box is slowly proving to be a formidable rival to Google classroom. This app enables students to easily work on and submit their class homework assignments to their teachers. Created by Colin Bramm and Roy Pombeiro, the app is used by three million teachers and students in 135 countries across the globe.

Smart homes

Torontonian Stuart Lombard founded ecobee in 2007 because he wanted a better way to conserve home energy and reduce his environmental footprint. Now the company is a world leader in smart-home services, with smart thermostats, cameras, sensors and home monitoring.

SIR FREDERICK BANTING

First Canadian Nobel Prize winner

You might be familiar with author Alice Munro, who was awarded the 2013 Nobel Prize in Literature, becoming the first Canadian to be so honoured. But do you know who was the first Canadian to win any Nobel Prize? That would be Sir Frederick Banting, who discovered insulin (along with his assistant, Charles Best, and other colleagues), thereby changing the lives of millions of people with diabetes. In 1923 — the year after he first injected a patient with insulin — he was awarded the Nobel Prize in Medicine. Here's a list of our other winners:

1.	Donna Strickland (1959–)	Physics, 2018
2.	Arthur B. McDonald (1943–)	Physics, 2015
3.	Alice Munro (1931–)	Literature, 2013
4.	Ralph Steinman (1943–2011)	Medicine, 2011
5.	Willard S. Boyle (1924–2011)	Physics, 2009
6.	Robert A. Mundell (1932–)	Economics, 1999
7.	Myron S. Scholes (1941–)	Economics, 1996
8.	William Vickrey (1914–96)	Economics, 1996
9.	Bertram N. Brockhouse (1918–2003)	Physics, 1994
10.	Michael Smith (1932–2000)	Chemistry, 1993
11.	Rudolph A. Marcus (1923–)	Chemistry, 1992
12.	Richard E. Taylor (1929–)	Physics, 1990
13.	Sidney Altman (1939–)	Chemistry, 1989
14.	John Polanyi (1929–)	Chemistry, 1986
15.	Henry Taube (1915–2005)	Chemistry, 1983
16.	David H. Hubel (1926–)	Medicine, 1981
17.	Saul Bellow* (1915–2005)	Literature, 1976
18.	Charles Brenton Huggins (1901–97)	Medicine, 1966
19.	Lester Bowles Pearson (1897–1972)	Peace, 1957
20.	William Francis Giauque (1895–1982)	Chemistry, 1949
21.	Frederick Grant Banting (1891–1941)	Medicine, 1923

*Saul Bellow was born in Quebec but later became an American citizen.

►► *Innovations* | Medicine

Artificial intelligence for drug creation

Deep Genomics is a Toronto-based tech company using AI to create genetic therapies that could be used to treat life-threatening disease.

Cobalt bomb

Medical physicist Dr. Harold Johns and his graduate students at the University of Saskatchewan were the first researchers to successfully treat a cancer patient using cobalt-60 radiation therapy, in 1951. The technology, also known as "the cobalt bomb," significantly changed cancer treatment and saved and prolonged the lives of millions of cancer patients.

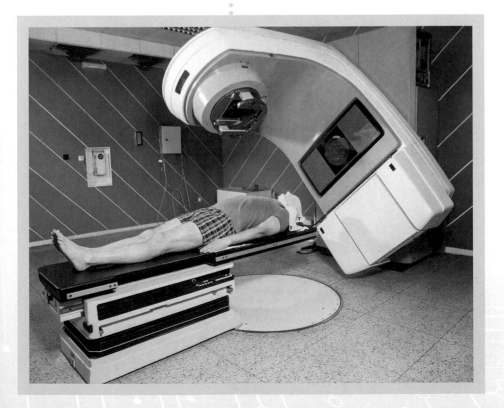

►► *Innovations* | **Medicine**

Mobile transfusion

Norman Bethune, born in Graven-hurst, Ontario, in 1890, devised the world's first mobile blood transfusion service during the early days of the Spanish War, which began in 1936. Blood was collected in cities and transported to the front lines. The service is considered the greatest innovation in military medicine to arise from that war.

Bethune rib shears

Bethune is also known for a number of medical innovations earlier in his career, while working near Montreal in the late 1920s and 1930s. Bethune pioneered numerous new medical techniques and instruments, one of which — the Bethune rib shears — is still manufactured.

NORMAN BETHUNE

Electric wheelchair

Born in Hamilton, Ontario, George Klein invented the electric wheelchair in 1955 while working for the National Research Council. Originally created for disabled military personnel, the first prototype of the joystick-controlled, battery-operated wheelchair was presented to the United States Veterans Administration.

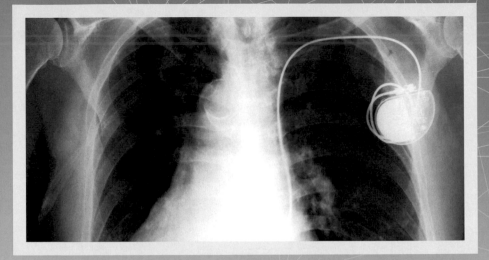

Electronic heart pacemaker

The electronic heart pacemaker was invented in 1949 by Dr. Wilfred Bigelow and Dr. John Callaghan of Toronto, with the help of electrical engineer John Hopps of the National Research Council in Ottawa. In 1958, Arne Larsson was the first person to have an implantable pacemaker. It lasted just three hours. During his lifetime, Larsson had 28 pacemakers before he died at the age of 86.

Mobile operating theatre

Bethune also created the globe's first mobile operating theatre, in 1938 while working for the Chinese Communist Party during the Second Sino-Japanese War. The facility, which could be carried by two donkeys, was put to good use. Bethune is reported to have operated on 115 soldiers during a 69-hour period without pause under heavy artillery fire.

Artificial kidney

In the 1940s, Dr. Gordon Murray of Toronto independently designed the first artificial kidney in North America, unaware that Willem Kolff was working in Holland on a similar invention. Kolff is considered the inventor of the dialysis machine, though the artificial kidneys in operation today are based more on Murray's methods. Dr. Murray's contributions to medicine didn't stop there, however: he was also the first to transplant a human heart valve.

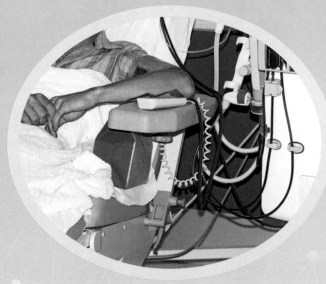

First surgery by robot

Dr. Mehran Anvari, a professor of surgery and the head of Minimally Invasive Surgery and Surgical Innovation at McMaster University in Hamilton, Ontario, performed the world's first telerobotic-assisted surgery. In 2003, he operated on a patient at North Bay Regional Health Centre from more than 400 km away, at St. Joseph's Healthcare Hamilton. He has since worked with the Canadian Space Agency and NASA on robotic surgical technologies.

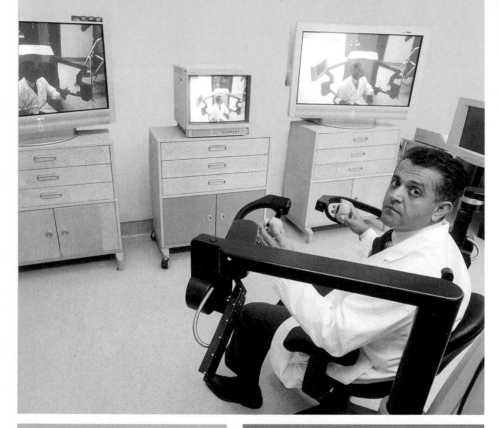

WEEVAC 6

Here's proof big things can come in small packages. The WEEVAC 6, the world's first evacuation stretcher designed for infants, was created in 1987 by Canadian Wendy Murphy.

T-cell receptor

This could get complicated, so let's keep things simple. In 1984, Canadian Dr. Tak Wah Mak co-discovered the T-cell receptor. This led doctors to a better understanding of how the immune system recognizes and fights infections, allowing them to create new, more effective drugs. The discovery is considered the Holy Grail of immunology.

First vaccination

Dr. John Clinch is believed to have been the first doctor in North America to administer vaccinations. In 1798, the first person he vaccinated was his nephew Joseph Hart. Clinch later vaccinated 700 people for smallpox in Trinity, Newfoundland. Encouraged by the results, doctors in other communities in the province and in Halifax adopted the practice.

►► *Innovations*
Communications

First submarine telegraph cable

The first submarine telegraph cable in North America was laid by Frederick N. Gisborne between New Brunswick and Prince Edward Island in 1852, most of it by a machine he devised himself. He also engineered the first link between Cape Breton and Cape Ray, Newfoundland, in 1856.

First transatlantic telephone cable

A cooperative effort of the General Post Office of the United Kingdom, American Telegraph and Telephone (AT&T) and the Canadian Overseas Telephone Corporation, TAT-1 was the first transatlantic telephone cable. Actually there were two cables, laid side by side (one running in each direction) in the summer of 1955 and 1956. TAT-1 linked Scotland near Oban to London and to Clarenville, Newfoundland, then across the Cabot Strait to Nova Scotia. TAT-1 was retired in the late 1970s. Shown here is a section of the cable stripped away to show its various layers.

First radio message

It's an apt name. Signal Hill in St. John's, Newfoundland, is the site where Guglielmo Marconi received the first transatlantic radio telegraphic message on December 12, 1901. Marconi and his assistant, George Kemp, used an antenna raised by a kite and listened, hoping to hear three clicks sent from a radio transmitter 3,500 km away in Poldhu, a small village on the southwest coast of England. After three days — *click-click-click* — they received the first Morse-code message ever to cross the Atlantic Ocean. The Tower at Signal Hill, now part of a national historic site, was used for signalling until 1960.

First trans-Canada telephone system

The first "trans-Canada" telephone system was completed in 1932. It covered Toronto, Montreal, Quebec City, Hamilton and Windsor.

First telegraph

Oh, how far we've come. The first electric telegraph message in Canada was sent on December 19, 1846. The early means of electronically sending encoded messages was used to communicate between Toronto City Hall and Hamilton on a line owned by the Toronto, Hamilton and Niagara Electric-Magnetic Telegraph Company. The transmission: "Advise Mr. Gamble [president of the telegraph company] that Mr. Dawson will speak to him at half-past one."

▶▶ *Innovations*
Communications

First trans-Canada broadcast
It was a special Canada Day. On July 1, 1927, Prime Minister Mackenzie King spoke to Canadians from Parliament Hill in the first trans-Canada radio broadcast. The milestone event included a variety of other speeches and performances in recognition of the Diamond Jubilee of Canada's Confederation.

First television broadcast
The first television pictures in Canada were broadcast in the summer of 1932, using the CKAC radio transmission in Montreal. The broadcasts were experimental and only a handful of people had receivers to view them on.

First voice radio transmission
Canadian-born inventer Reginald Fessenden is credited with the first achievement in the creation of what is now radio. On December 23, 1900, he sent the world's first wireless transmission of a human voice at Cobb Island, Maryland. The signal, sent via electromagnetic waves, travelled about 1.5 km.

First smartphone
The Blackberry phone is considered the pioneer of the modern smartphone that we know and love today. Founded by Mike Lazaridis and Doug Fregin in Waterloo, Ontario, in 1984, the company released its first smartphone, the Blackberry 5810, in 2002. The phone immediately became the most-used technology device by companies, and not soon after, the general public also flocked to the phone. Blackberry ruled the smartphone world until 2007. For the next few years, the company battled it out for the bulk of the industry's consumers, and while Apple and Samsung overtook Blackberry to dominate the smartphone market, many customers remained loyal to the Blackberry — former president Barack Obama did not give up his until 2016.

First phone call

Alexander Graham Bell was a man of many firsts, not the least of which was making the first one-way, long-distance telephone calls between the Ontario communities of Brantford and Paris, and Mount Pleasant and Brantford, on August 10, 1876. Bell received that first call from Brantford in Robert White's Boot and Shoe Store and Telegram Office in Paris.

First emergency-services number

Who doesn't know the phone number 911 and what it's for? But did you know that Winnipeg was the first city in North America to implement a central phone number to contact emergency services? The number (the city used 999 at the time) was introduced on June 21, 1959, at the suggestion of Winnipeg mayor Stephen Juba. Most of North America adopted 911 as the emergency contact number on June 22, 1975.

10

Money Stuff

Ink for "greenbacks"

Who'd have thought that the distinct green-coloured ink that is used to make American bills was developed in Canada. Thomas Sterry Hunt invented the anti-counterfeit ink while working as a professor at Laval University in Montreal, Quebec. In 1857, Hunt, a chemist who was a member of the Geological Survey of Canada, began experimenting with chromium to find an ink for bank notes that would be hard to reproduce. In his experiments, Hunt discovered chromium trioxide, which was hard to remove from paper money, and in 1862, it was adopted by the United States Treasury Department to ink all the country's bank notes.

The Hockey Sweater

Roch Carrier's timeless story, *Le Chandail de Hockey* (The Hockey Sweater), is so cherished by Canadians that an excerpt of the story was depicted on the Canadian $5 bill for a decade, from 2002 to 2012. This story, about a hockey-obsessed child from small-town Quebec who is forced to wear (of all things) a Toronto Maple Leafs jersey, rather than a jersey from his beloved team, the Montreal Canadiens, still resonates with Canadians today.

First coin

The first domestically produced Canadian coin was struck on January 2, 1908, at the opening ceremony for the Royal Mint in Ottawa. The silver 50-cent piece bore the effigy of King Edward VII.

First $1 million coin

Don't try making change for this coin. The Royal Canadian Mint created the world's first $1 million coin in 2007. The 100 kg, 99999 (99.999 percent) pure gold bullion coin was created to market the Mint's new standard for gold coin purity. However, a number of people came forward interested in purchasing the real McCoy. The Mint has subsequently sold five of the colossal coins, which at the time were the world's largest.

Pure gold coin 1

In 1982, the Royal Canadian Mint's refinery produced the world's first 9999 (99.9 percent pure) gold bullion coins — the Gold Maple Leaf coin.

Pure gold coin 2

In 2007, the Royal Canadian Mint one-upped itself by producing the world's first 99999 (99.999 percent pure) gold bullion coin. It is the only mint in the world to produce coins at this standard.

Royal Canadian Mint

What do Cuba's centavos, Yemen's fils, Colombia's pesos, and Iceland's krona all have in common? These are all coins that are produced right here in Canada — in Winnipeg to be specific. Not only does the Royal Canadian mint in Winnipeg produce all of Canada's coin currency, over the last 25 years it has also produced coins for more than 60 different countries.

11

Boats, Trains, Autos & Planes

First solo voyage around the world

Joshua Slocum, a native of Annapolis County, Nova Scotia, became the first person to sail solo around the world. He departed from Boston for the 74,000 km voyage on April 24, 1895, in his ship the *Spray*; the trip took three years to complete. His book on the journey, *Sailing Alone around the World*, has been continuously in print since it was published in 1900.

Northwest Passage (E-W)

Norwegian explorer Roald Amundsen was the first person to navigate Canada's Northwest Passage, a water route from the Atlantic to the Pacific Ocean through Canada's Arctic Archipelago, by ship, from 1903 to 1906. Amundsen sailed his ship *Gjoa* west and south of Lancaster Sound through Peel Sound and through Queen Maud and Coronation gulfs in the western Arctic.

Northwest Passage (W-E)

The RCMP auxiliary schooner *St. Roch* holds a special place (or two or three!) in Canadian maritime history. Designed to avoid being crushed by ice, the wooden, sail-powered *St. Roch* was the first ship to sail the Northwest Passage from west to east, from 1941 to 1942. The ship was trapped in the ice for two seasons before it completed its journey on October 11, 1942.

Northwest Passage (E-W in one season)

The *St. Roch* was the first vessel to travel the Northwest Passage in one season, which it did, east to west, in 1944, between July 22 and October 16. It travelled a new route, sailing through Lancaster Sound, through Prince of Wales Strait and along the northern Alaska coast.

Northwest Passage both ways

Thanks to its two voyages through the Northwest Passage (1941–42 and 1944), the *St. Roch* became the first ship to sail the legendary route in both directions.

Circumnavigating North America

To complete its maritime milestones, the *St. Roch* also became the first ship to circumnavigate North America, in 1950.

Northwest Passage (W-E in one season)

The HMCS *Labrador*, an icebreaker of the Royal Canadian Navy, was the first vessel to travel the Northwest Passage west to east in a single season, in 1954.

▶▶ *Boats, Trains, Autos & Planes*

First Canadian steamboat
John Molson, founder of the Molson brewery, was responsible for the construction of the first entirely Canadian-made steamboat in 1809, *The Accommodation*. Molson eventually extended the endeavour to a fleet of 22 ships. The venture helped open the St. Lawrence and Canada to trade and settlement.

Free ferry
Looking for a free ride? Try British Columbia's Kootenay Lake Ferry, the world's longest free ferry ride. There are actually two ferries that run year-round between Kootenay Bay and Balfour, a 35-minute trip. Both vessels — the *Osprey 2000* and the *MV Balfour* — accommodate vehicles of all sizes, including RVs.

First steamship across the Atlantic

The SS *Royal William* was the first Canadian ship to cross the Atlantic completely under steam power. It was first launched in Quebec on April 27, 1831. Later that year, the ship made several voyages between Quebec and Atlantic Canada, but in 1832 it was quarantined because of a cholera epidemic. On August 18, 1833, with seven passengers and a load of coal, it started the 25-day journey from Pictou, Nova Scotia, to Gravesend, England. The ship was eventually sold to the Spanish Navy.

First trip across the Atlantic in a raft

It sounds almost too crazy to be true, but it really happened! On May 24, 1956, Henri Beaudout and his crew of three novice sailors launched from Halifax on a raft made from little more than nine telephone poles tied together with 2 km of rope. The crew hoped to be the first to cross the frigid Atlantic via raft. Beaudout's bet was that they would eventually enter the Gulf Stream and be whisked across the ocean by the current. The raft, *L'Égaré II* (meaning "the lost one"), landed in Falmouth, England, on August 21, 1956, 89 harrowing days after launch.

Northernmost shipwreck

In 1980, Dr. Joseph MacInnis (see page 44) led the team that discovered the world's northernmost shipwreck. On August 13, the remains of the SS *Breadalbane* — a Royal Navy ship that sank in August 1853 while delivering supplies to another expedition — were found by MacInnis' crew near Nunavut's Beechy Island.

▶▶ *Boats, Trains,*
Autos & Planes

First transborder railway

The Grand Trunk Railway, incorporated in 1852, was the first transborder railway in North America. It ran from Sarnia, Ontario, to Portland, Maine. Trains began running from Montreal to Portland on the route in 1853.

Longest railway tunnel

Yes, there is a light at the end of the tunnel. Canada is home to the longest railway tunnel in North America, the 14.7 km Mount MacDonald Tunnel in British Columbia's Selkirk Mountains. Construction of the tunnel was completed in 1988.

First transcontinental train

On June 28, 1886, the country's first transcontinental train left Montreal for Port Moody, British Columbia. It arrived on July 4.

First train

Canada's first railway was opened in 1836 between La Prairie and Saint-Jean-sur-Richelieu, Quebec. It was called the Champlain and St. Lawrence Railroad, since it connected the St. Lawrence River to Lake Champlain. On July 21, 1836, a Dorchester locomotive pulled two coaches from La Prairie to Saint-Jean-sur-Richelieu and back.

First submarine tunnel

The world's first international submarine tunnel, linking Sarnia, Ontario, with Port Huron, Michigan, opened on September 19, 1891. The St. Clair Tunnel, almost 2 km long, was used by the Grand Trunk Railroad.

▶▶ *Boats, Trains, Autos & Planes*

First electric car

The buzz these days over electric cars seems a little funny when you consider the nation's first electric car was built more than 100 years ago, in 1893. Frederick B. Featherstonhaugh [left] commissioned the Dixon Carriage Works to build it, using a battery and motor designed by William Still. The two-person car was capable of about 25 km per hour.

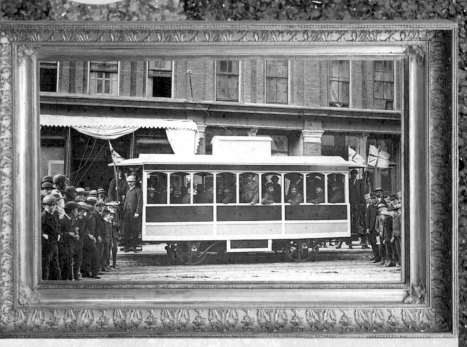

First streetcar

The first commercial electric streetcar service in Canada began in Windsor, Ontario, on May 28, 1886. The Windsor Electric Railway had just 2.4 km of track.

First gas car

The first successful gasoline-powered car in Canada was built by George Foote Foss in Sherbrooke, Quebec, in 1896. Its name? The Fossmobile!

First electric transit system

Windsor, Ontario, was the nation's first city with an all-electric transit system. That was inaugurated in 1891, when the city' Sandwich & Windsor Passenger Railway — a series of horse-drawn carts running on rails — was converted to a streetcar system.

First car

The first car manufactured in Canada was the Taylor Steam Buggy, built by Henry Seth Taylor of Stanstead, Quebec, in 1867. The car was powered by a coil-fired boiler at the back and used a handle to control its speed and a horizontal bar to steer.

First trolley bus

Windsor, Ontario, boasted the country's first trolley bus (a trackless electric system run by an overhead wire), which debuted on May 4, 1922.

▶▶ *Boats, Trains, Autos & Planes*

First pilot

He wasn't the first in North America, but Frederick Baldwin was the first Canadian to pilot a plane. On March 12, 1908, at Hammondsport, New York, he flew a plane called the *Red Wing*, a biplane with the propeller located behind the wing. It flew a distance of 97.2 m before flipping to its side and crashing.

First airplane

The *Baddeck No. 1* was the first made-in-Canada powered aircraft. Built by the Canadian Aerodrome Company, its first flight was on August 12, 1909.

First Canadian flight

The first flight in Canada occurred in Baddeck, Nova Scotia, on February 23, 1909. The silver-winged biplane, called the *Silver Dart*, was piloted by J.A.D. McCurdy. It flew 800 m at an average speed of 65 km per hour. The *Silver Dart* flew 200 flights before it was damaged beyond repair.

First airship

The R-100 airship was the first and only rigid-hull airship to ever fly in Canada. After a four-day flight from England, the airship moored at Saint-Hubert, Quebec, on August 1, 1930. It's estimated that more than one million people went to see it there.

First sounding rocket

The Black Brant sounding rocket, invented in the 1950s, was the first industrial-scale rocket built in Canada. A high-altitude rocket typically used to launch research instruments, the first was launched in September 1959 from Fort Churchill, Manitoba. The Black Brant is still used today by both the Canadian Space Agency and NASA.

First water bomber

It figures that the only plane in the world built specifically to fight forest fires would be Canadian. The Canadair CL-215 was the world's first amphibious water bomber. Its first flight was October 23, 1967. The plane features two 2,271-litre tanks, which take 8 to 10 seconds to scoop water and just two seconds to dump.

▶▶ *Boats, Trains, Autos & Planes*

First flight over Rockies

The first flight over the Canadian Rocky Mountains occurred on August 7, 1919. Pilot Ernest Hoy flew a Curtiss JN-4 from Vancouver to Calgary. The flight took 16.5 hours.

First trans-Canada flight

The first trans-Canada flight took 10 days. It began on October 7, 1920, in Halifax and involved five different planes and six pilots. The journey ended in Richmond, British Columbia. It was also Canada's first transcontinental airmail run, as packages were dropped off (literally in some cases!) along the route.

First non-stop trans-Canada flight

On January 15, 1949, the first non-stop trans-Canada flight, from Vancouver to Halifax, took place. A Canadair North Star airplane took eight and a half hours to make the flight.

MILITARY EXPERIMENTS AT MONTREAL AVIATION MEET

Department May Test the Practicability of Aeroplanes in War Time. Officials Will Be Sent Down To Witness the Maneuvers and Dragoons From Farnham Will Patrol the Aviation Field. McCurdy Arrives With His Flier.

It is announced at the militia department that the government will be officially represented at the forthcoming aviation meet to be held in Montreal, starting June 25 and continuing until June 4. Officials will be present, and will conduct a series of experiments with some of the aerial craft entered in the competitions. Engineers versed in war strategy will probably test the value of the aeroplanes by shooting from them and letting bombs fall, reporting to the department the result of their experiments.

Col. F. L. Lessard has wired the of-

act as his assistants in making the experiments.

It is also probable that Major Maunsell of the engineering branch, will attend the meet in an official capacity. Major Maunsell has shown his interest already in experimenting with aeroplanes, having visited Baddeck, N.S., this spring, where Baldwin and McCurdy were giving trial exhibitions with their aerodrome. It has been announced that McCurdy will be at the Montreal meet and as the government are known to be considering a grant to these Canadian aviators, it is not unlikely that their machines will be used in whatever experiments are made for the militia department. A despatch from Montreal today

First aviation meet

On June 25, 1910, Canada's first aviation meet (and the largest in North America at the time) took flight. The Montreal Aviation Meet boasted 10 airplanes and nine pilots.

First intercity flight

The first intercity flight in Canada took place in 1911, when famed pilot J.A.D McCurdy won an airplane race from Hamilton to Toronto — after giving his competitors a 10-minute head start.

Firsts in aviation

J.A.D. McCurdy was a man of many firsts.
Some highlights:

▶ He performed the first figure-eight manoeuvre in an airplane in the world on August 28, 1908.
▶ He co-founded the first aircraft manufacturing company in Canada, The Canadian Aerodrome Company, in April 1909.
▶ He was the first Canadian to be issued a pilot's licence.
▶ He established the first aviation school in Canada.
▶ He was the first to fly a "flying boat," on May 1, 1910.
▶ He was the first to attempt to fly an airplane across the ocean from Key West, Florida, to Havana, Cuba, in 1911 — and he almost made it too, crashing not far from the coast of Cuba.

Aviation license firsts

Roland J. Groome was also a man of firsts. Along with Edward Clarke and Bob McCombie, Groome formed the Aerial Service Company in 1919 and built the first licensed aerodrome in Canada in Regina, Saskatchewan. Groome would become the first licensed commercial aviator in the nation. One of the company's aircrafts became the country's first licensed commercial airplane: the Curtiss JN-4 Canuck.

First jetliner

The Avro Canada C102 Jetliner was a first in many respects. Built by Avro Canada in 1949, it was the first Canadian jet to fly and the first commercial jet in North America (and the second in the world: just two weeks behind the first!). The prototype jet's first flight was over Toronto's Malton Airport on August 10, 1949. The following year, the plane was the first to make an airmail delivery by jet on April 18, 1950, on a flight from Toronto to New York.

First bush pilot

Bush flying was hugely important to the early days of exploring Canada's vast hinterland. It started out as a means to spot forest fires. Stuart Graham was the first to fly such patrols over Quebec's St. Maurice River Valley in 1919, in two war-surplus Curtiss HS-2L flying boats. Thus began a key method of accessing the country's more remote regions.

First forest fire spotted from the air

Fire! On July 7, 1919, Stuart Graham and Bill Kahre became the first to spot a forest fire in Canada from the air, while they were flying over Quebec's St. Maurice River.

First bush plane

The bush plane is synonymous with Canada's hinterland. The first successful, all-Canadian bush plane was the Noorduyn Norseman, which first flew in November 1935. More than 900 were built in Montreal by its designer, R.B.C. Noorduyn. The aircraft's large cabin and its ability to take off and land in tight spots made the plane a sought-after workhorse. The one pictured here was used by the U.S. Forest Service.

►► *Boats, Trains, Autos & Planes*

First metal bush plane

The de Havilland DHC-2 Beaver was the first all-metal bush plane designed and built in Canada. It was particularly well known for its ability on short takeoffs and landings. More Beavers were built than any other Canadian aircraft to date: 1,692 between 1947 and 1968.

Building Canada
A Timeline of Historical Events

12,000 to 30,000 years ago:

The first people — the ancestors of Canada's Indigenous peoples — cross over into Canada. Today the term Indigenous peoples refers to three groups: First Nation, Inuit and Métis. The Inuit, which means "the people" in the Inuktitut language, live in communities across the Arctic. The Métis are a distinct people of combined Indigenous and European ancestry who come from both French- and English-speaking backgrounds.

About 1,000 years ago:

Leif Erikson leads a Viking expedition to the New World. The remains of a Viking settlement, L'Anse aux Meadows, in Newfoundland and Labrador, are a World Heritage Site.

1451 The Haudenosaunee Confederacy

The Haudenosaunee (Iroquois) Confederacy is formed. Originally a group of five nations living in the northern part of New York state, the Haudenosaunee nations were the Seneca, Cayuga, Oneida, Onondaga and Mohawk. In the 1700s the Tuscarora joined and the confederacy became known as the Six Nations.

1497 John Cabot

Italian-born explorer John Cabot leads an English expedition to what is thought to have been Newfoundland and Labrador or Cape Breton Island. He claims the continent for the King of England.

1534-42 Jacques Cartier

Jacques Cartier makes three voyages across the Atlantic, claiming the land for France. In 1535, he becomes the first European to sail into the St. Lawrence River. Cartier hears two First Nation guides talk about the route to "Kanata," the Haudenosaunee word for "village" or "settlement," and by 1547 maps designate everything north of the St. Lawrence as "Canada."

JOHN CABOT

1576 Martin Frobisher

In search of the Northwest Passage to Asia, British explorer Martin Frobisher reaches Baffin Island in what is now Nunavut.

1604 Pierre Dugua de Mons

Explorer Pierre Dugua de Mons and his expedition (which included Samuel de Champlain) attempts to establish the first French settlement in North America on Saint Croix Island, which lies on the United States' side of the St. Croix River, between Maine and New Brunswick. But frigid temperatures that year made it difficult for the group to reach the mainland, where game and fresh water were abundant, and so the settlement was moved to Annapolis Royal (then called Port-Royal), Nova Scotia.

1608 Samuel de Champlain

Samuel de Champlain sets up a fur-trading post at the site of what is now Quebec City — Canada's oldest city.

1642 Montreal

Montreal is founded as a mission and becomes a base for the fur trade.

MARTIN FROBISHER

Pierre Dugua de Mons   Canada 49

FLAG OF MONTREAL

SAMUEL DE CHAMPLAIN

►► *Building Canada*
A Timeline of Historical Events

ACADIAN FLAG

1670 Hudson's Bay Company

The Hudson's Bay Company is established to trade for furs in what is today northern and western Canada. In 1690, Henry Kelsey, a Hudson's Bay Company fur trader, becomes the first European to see the western prairies. The photo here shows a Hudson's Bay Company store in Calgary in 1884.

1713 Treaty of Utrecht

The Treaty of Utrecht leaves Hudson Bay, Acadia and Newfoundland to Britain, and Cape Breton and St. John's Island (now Prince Edward Island) to France. (Acadia, founded in 1604, was a region first settled by France in present-day Nova Scotia, New Brunswick, Prince Edward Island and the coastal area from the St. Lawrence River south into Maine.)

1755 Acadian expulsion

The expulsion of the Acadians begins. About 10,000 Acadians who refuse to pledge allegiance to the British Crown must forfeit their property and are forced to leave the region. Many wind up in what is now Louisiana, and over time the Acadians there become the Cajuns.

THE DEATH OF GENERAL WOLFE (1770), BY BENJAMIN WEST

1756 Seven Years' War

The Seven Years' War begins in North America and then spreads to Europe as Britain declares war on France.

1759 Quebec City (New France) falls

Quebec City falls to the British following the Battle of the Plains of Abraham. This is the key battle for North America and marks the end of France's empire in America. The commanders of both armies — Brigadier General James Wolfe and the Marquis de Montcalm — are both killed leading their troops in battle.

1763 Treaty of Paris
1774 The Quebec Act

The Seven Years' War ends with the Treaty of Paris. New France is formally ceded to Britain. The Quebec Act restores French laws and institutions in Quebec and extends the provincial boundary.

►► *Building Canada*
A Timeline of Historical Events

1791 Upper and Lower Canada
The Province of Quebec is divided into two separate colonies — Upper Canada (roughly today's southern Ontario), in the western portion of the province, and Lower Canada (roughly today's southern Quebec), in the eastern portion. The Town of York (now Toronto) is established as the capital of Upper Canada.

1783 Loyalists arrive
Loyalists (American colonists who supported the British during the American Revolution) begin to arrive in what are now the Maritime provinces, Ontario and Quebec. About 30,000 will eventually flee to Canada.

1783 Treaty of Paris
The Treaty of Paris officially marks the end of the War of American Independence as Great Britain recognizes the sovereignty of the United States. According to the terms of the treaty, the United States is granted a clearly defined border with Canada and the equal partition of the Great Lakes, except for Lake Michigan, which is granted to the Americans in full.

LOYALISTS FLAG

1848–49
Responsible government formed

Reformers such as Louis-Hippolyte Lafontaine and Robert Baldwin work together toward responsible government. Under responsible government, the support of the majority of elected representatives is required. This system, which is responsible to the people, is the one that Canada has today.

1841
Province of Canada

Upper Canada (renamed Canada West) and Lower Canada (renamed Canada East) are united as the Province of Canada. In 1857, Queen Victoria chooses Ottawa to be the capital for the Province of Canada. Although it is a logging town far from the colony's main cities, it is the only sizable settlement located on the border of Canada East and Canada West.

1837–38 British rebellions

Rebellions against British rule take place in Upper and Lower Canada.

1812–15
The War of 1812

The War of 1812 begins as U.S. forces invade Canada. The attempt to conquer Canada fails as the result of the efforts of Canada's volunteers and First Nations, supported by British soldiers. The present-day Canada–U.S. border is partly a result of that war.

WAR OF 1812 BATTLE OF QUEENSTON HEIGHTS (1896), BY JOHN DAVID KELLY

THE UNDERGROUND RAILROAD (1893), BY CHARLES T. WEBBER

1850–60
The Underground Railroad

As the debate over the abolition of slavery intensified in the United States, thousands of slaves escape from the United States and reach Canada by way of the Underground Railroad, a secret network for fugitive slaves.

1853–54
First through the Northwest Passage

Canada's Northwest Passage has long transfixed explorers searching for a navigable route across the top of North America. In 1853–54, British explorer Robert McClure was the first recorded person to complete the route, partly by sledge, from west to east.

1869
Canada buys Rupert's Land

The Hudson's Bay Company sells Rupert's Land to the Government of Canada but fails to consider the existing residents — mainly Métis and First Nations. The Métis of the Red River Colony are concerned that they will lose their land rights and culture. Under Louis Riel (pictured above) they mount a rebellion which later becomes known as the North-West Rebellion.

▶▶ Building Canada

1864-67
Confederation: Canada is born

In 1864, representatives of Nova Scotia, New Brunswick and the Province of Canada work to establish a new country. These men, known as the Fathers of Confederation, create two levels of government — federal and provincial. The Province of Canada is split into two new provinces — Ontario and Quebec — which, with New Brunswick and Nova Scotia, form the Dominion of Canada. In 1867, the British Parliament passes the British North America Act, and the Dominion of Canada is officially born on July 1. John A. Macdonald is selected the country's first prime minister.

1870-1949
Expansion of Canada

Between 1870 and 1873, the North-West Territories and the provinces of Manitoba, British Columbia, and Prince Edward Island officially join Canada. Yukon is split from the North-West Territories in 1898 and enters Confederation. In 1905, the provinces of Alberta and Saskatchewan also leave the North-West Territories to join Canada, followed by Newfoundland in 1949.

1914-18
The War to End all Wars

The First World War. Canada makes great contributions but suffers great losses, with more than 60,000 dead and 170,000 wounded. More than 650,000 Canadians and Newfound-landers (Newfoundland was not yet a province) serve in the war, out of a population of only eight million. The Canadian Corps captures Vimy Ridge in 1917 — a major victory over German forces, but at a great cost, with more than 10,000 killed and wounded.

A Timeline of Historical Events

1885
First transcontinental railway

The nation's first transcontinental railway, the Canadian Pacific Railway, was completed on November 7, 1885. The last spike was driven in at Craigellachie, British Columbia.

1918
First secret sitting of Parliament

Keep it on the down low. On April 17, 1918, the House of Commons held its first secret sitting. Members were told that Allied forces in Europe faced possible defeat.

1885
North-West Rebellion ends

The five-month-long North-West Rebellion, fought mainly by Métis and their First Nations allies against the Canadian government, and led by Louis Riel, is forcibly ended. Louis Riel is hanged for high treason.

1916-51
Women's right to vote

Women win the right to vote in Manitoba, Saskatchewan and Alberta in 1916. They win the right in the other provinces and territories in 1917 (British Columbia and Ontario); 1918 (Nova Scotia); 1919 (New Brunswick and Yukon); 1922 (Prince Edward Island); 1925 (Newfoundland and Labrador); 1940 (Quebec); and 1951 (Northwest Territories). At the time of Confederation, the vote was limited to property-owning white males. The effort by women to achieve the right to vote is known as the women's suffrage movement. Its founder in Canada was Dr. Emily Stowe, the first woman to practise medicine in the country.

1929-39
The Great Depression

The Great Depression — a period of severe economic hardship — finds up to 25 percent of the Canadian labour force out of work.

Emily Stowe

CANADA postage postes 17

▶▶ *Building Canada*
A Timeline of Historical Events

1939-45
The Second World War
The Canadian military plays an important role in the war, with action in Dieppe, France; the invasion of Italy; D-Day landings; the liberation of the Netherlands; and the final defeat of Germany. In 1941, The federal government allows women to enlist in the army in support roles. More than one million Canadians and Newfoundlanders serve in the military — over 45,000 give their lives, and another 55,000 are wounded.

1944
Health care
T.C. (Tommy) Douglas leads the Co-operative Commonwealth Federation to power in Saskatchewan. He introduces the universal health-insurance system that would eventually be adopted across Canada.

1942
Japanese internment
The Canadian government announces plans to move all Canadians of Japanese origin on the country's west coast to inland camps. Their property is sold without compensation. In 1988, the Canadian government apologized and compensated the victims.

1959
St. Lawrence Seaway

The St. Lawrence Seaway — a system of canals, dams and locks — is completed. It stretches for 3,790 km inland from the Atlantic Ocean to Lake Superior and is the world's longest inland waterway connected to ocean shipping.

1960
The Quiet Revolution | Indigenous peoples can vote | Bill of Rights

The Canadian Bill of Rights, setting out the rights of Canadians, becomes law. Indigenous peoples are granted the right to vote in federal elections without losing their treaty status. "The Quiet Revolution" — a period of political, social and educational changes — begins in Quebec. Premier Jean Lesage is a figurehead for the movement.

1962
Trans-Canada Highway

The Trans-Canada Highway, which today links St. John's in Newfoundland with Victoria in British Columbia, opens at British Columbia's Rogers Pass. At 7,821 km, it is one of the world's longest highways

►► *Building Canada*
A Timeline of Historical Events

1967
Canada's big birthday
Canada celebrates the 100th anniversary of Confederation and hosts Expo 67 in Montreal. The World's Fair attracts more than 50 million visitors.

1969
Official Languages Act
The Official Languages Act comes into force, declaring English and French as the official languages of Canada.

1965
Canadian flag
After months of debate, Canada adopts the maple leaf flag.

L'Exposition universelle de 1967—
Le Spectacle du Siècle
The 1967 World Exhibition—
Show of the Century

expo67
29 AVRIL–27 OCTOBRE ■ APRIL 28–OCTOBER 27

MONTREAL CANADA

▶▶ *Building Canada*
A Timeline of Historical Events

1980
Canada's anthem
"O Canada" is officially proclaimed the national anthem, 100 years after it was first sung. In 2018, the anthem was made gender neutral with the lyric "in all thy sons command" officially replaced with "in all of us command."

1982
Canada's Charter of Rights and Freedoms
Canada adopts its Constitution, with a Charter of Rights and Freedoms. Among the rights found in the Charter are freedom of conscience and religion; Indigenous peoples' rights; and mobility rights (the right of each citizen to enter, remain in and leave Canada).

1994
NAFTA
Canada, the United States and Mexico sign the North American Free Trade Agreement (NAFTA). NAFTA is replaced with the new United States-Mexico-Canada trade agreement (USMCA) in 2020.

1999
Territory of Nunavut

Nunavut, the eastern part of the Northwest Territories, officially becomes a self-governing territory. Iqaluit, previously called Frobisher Bay, is its capital.

1997
Confederation Bridge

Confederation Bridge opens, linking Prince Edward Island and New Brunswick. At a cost of $840 million, it is the longest bridge in the world (12.9 km) crossing ice-covered water.

1995
Quebec Referendum

A referendum is called in Quebec, in which the citizens of the province were to vote to either leave Canada or remain as part of the nation. The referendum was narrowly won by those in Quebec who wished to remain a part of Canada.

▶▶ *Building Canada*
A Timeline of Historical Events

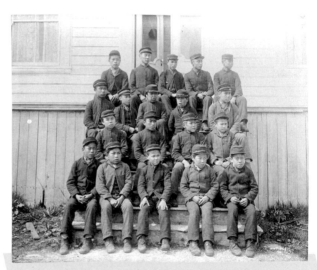

2003–05
The Michaels
Michael Leshner and Michael Stark become the first legally wed same-sex couple in Canada. The couple married in 2003 immediately after an Ontario court of appeal deemed it legal to do so. In 2005, the federal government passes legislation to recognize same-sex marriages, becoming the fourth nation to do so.

2008–15
Apology for Residential Schools
The federal government apologizes to Indigenous peoples for the residential school program it ran. Residential schools were government-sponsored religious schools aimed at converting Indigenous peoples to European-centric Canadian culture. An estimated 150,000 First Nation, Inuit and Métis children were forced to attended residential schools. In 2015 the Truth and Reconciliation Commission of Canada releases its final report covering residential schools. The report outlines steps to restore friendship and harmony among all Canadians and recommends 94 calls to action for the federal government.

2016
Fort McMurray fires

In May 2016, one of Canada's worst wildfires ravaged the northern Albertan community of Fort McMurray. More than 80,000 residents were evacuated and nearly 2,400 structures (almost 10 percent of the city) were destroyed. The fire was the most expensive natural disaster in Canadian history, costing insurance companies $3.7 billion.

2015–16
Coming to Canada

Canada resettles more than 25,000 Syrian refugees fleeing civil war in their country. Life is hard for many, but some, like Assam Hadhad and his family, who now call Antigonish, Nova Scotia, home, start successful businesses. The Hadhad family chocolate business, Peace by Chocolate, which started in the family's shed, opened its first factory in 2017.

2014–16
Franklin discovery

Explorer Sir John Franklin and his crew of 134 departed from England in May of 1845 aboard two ships, the HMS *Erebus* and the HMS *Terror*. Their quest was to uncover the yet uncharted portions of the Northwest Passage. Franklin's expedition, after being spotted that July near Baffin Bay, was never seen again. In 2014, researchers find the HMS *Erebus* off the coast of King William Island. In 2016 the HMS *Terror* is found in Nunavut's Terror Bay.

2010
Olympic victory

Canada hosts its third Olympic Games, this time in Vancouver (previous Games were held in Montreal, 1976, and Calgary, 1988). Before the Vancouver Games, a Canadian had not won an Olympic gold medal on home soil. Worry not! In Vancouver, Canada snags 14 of them — the most gold by any nation in any Winter Games!

13 ▶ *Guiding Canada*
Prime Ministers

John Alexander Macdonald (1815–1891)
Terms: 1867–73, 1878–91
Birthplace: Glasgow, Scotland
Political party: Liberal-
Conservative Party

Did you know?
The nation's first prime minister served for 19 years, during which time he oversaw major successes and controversies, including the execution of Louis Riel.

Alexander Mackenzie (1822–1892)
Term: 1873–78
Birthplace: Logierait, Scotland
Political party: Liberal Party of Canada

Did you know?
Canada's second prime minister oversaw the creation of the Supreme Court of Canada and the Auditor General's office. He also helped to build the nation's modern electoral system — the way in which Canadians vote for their leaders today.

John Joseph Caldwell Abbott (1821–1893)
Term: 1891-92
Birthplace: Saint-André-d'Argenteuil, Lower Canada (now Quebec)
Political party: Conservative Party

Did you know?
Prior to becoming prime minister, Abbott was instrumental in the planning and development of the Canadian Pacific Railway.

John Sparrow David Thompson (1845–1894)

Term: 1892–94
Birthplace: Halifax, Nova Scotia
Political party: Conservative Party

Did you know?

Thompson was a former attorney general for Nova Scotia. During his time as prime minister, Thompson's justice department drafted the Canadian Criminal Code of 1892 — the first of its kind in a self-governing British territory.

Mackenzie Bowell (1823–1917)

Term: 1894–96
Birthplace: Rickinghall, Suffolk, England
Political party: Conservative Party

Did you know?

At the time of Prime Minister Thompson's death in 1894, Bowell was a senator. Bowell was appointed by the Governor General to assume the role and duties of the prime minister in the interim. As he continued to hold his senate position during his appointment, Bowell did not serve in Parliament while prime minister.

Charles Tupper (1821–1915)

Term: 1896
Birthplace: Amherst, Nova Scotia
Political party: Conservative Party

Did you know?

Tupper was responsible for the legislation that brought Nova Scotia into the Dominion of Canada in 1867.

>> *Guiding Canada*
Prime Ministers

Wilfrid Laurier (1841–1919)

Term: 1896–1911
Birthplace: Saint-Lin, Canada East
Political party: Liberal Party

Did you know? Laurier was the nation's first French-
Canadian prime minister. He was an advocate for clemency
for Louis Riel and for reconciliation efforts between French
and English Canada.

Robert Laird Borden (1854–1937)

Terms: 1911–17, 1917–20
Birthplace: Grand Pré, Nova Scotia
Political parties: Conservative Party (1911-
1917), Union Party (1917-1920)

Did you know? Robert Borden solidified
Canada's identity as an autonomous nation by
insisting that Canada have its own represen-
tation at the signing of the Treaty of Versailles
in 1919, the peace agreement that brought
World War I to an end.

Arthur Meighen (1874–1960)

Terms: 1920–21, 1926
Birthplace: Anderson, Ontario
Political party: Conservative Party

Did you know? In 1921, Meighen's cabinet
crafted legislation to recognize Armistice Day (now
observed as Remembrance Day on November 11).

William Lyon Mackenzie King (1874–1950)

Terms: 1921–26, 1926–30, 1935–48
Birthplace: Berlin (Kitchener), Ontario
Political party: Liberal

Did you know? King deftly guided the country through the Great Depression and then the Second World War. While he led the nation with a steady hand, in his personal life, King was certainly colourful; his diary entries from 1893 to 1950 painted a picture of a man who was interested in magic and the occult — from seances with his dead mother and dead dog to checking his crystal ball before making major decisions. In spite of his quirky character, King is still revered by many as the greatest prime minister of this nation.

Richard Bedford Bennett (1870–1947)

Term: 1930–35
Birthplace: Hopewell, New Brunswick
Political party: Conservative Party

Did you know? Bennett created the Bank of Canada and the Canadian Radio Broadcasting Corporation (CRBC), now the Canadian Broadcasting Corporation (CBC).

Louis Stephen St-Laurent (1882–1973)

Term: 1948–57
Birthplace: Compton, Quebec
Political party: Liberal Party

Did you know? "Uncle Louis," as Louis St-Laurent came to be known, had an uncanny ability to connect with everyday Canadians. His platform was centred on national unity. In 1949, St-Laurent secured Newfoundland's entry into Confederation as Canada's 10th province.

John George Diefenbaker (1895–1979)

Term: 1957–63
Birthplace: Neustadt, Ontario
Political party: Progressive Conservative Party

Did you know? Diefenbaker appointed Canada's first woman cabinet minister, Ellen Fairclough, in 1957 and the first Indigenous senator, James Gladstone, in 1958. In 1958, Diefenbaker also introduced the Canadian Bill of Rights, and the following year he introduced legislation that allowed Canada's Indigenous peoples the right to vote.

Lester Bowles Pearson (1897–1972)

Term: 1963–68
Birthplace: Newtonbrook, Ontario
Political party: Liberal Party

Did you know? Before he became prime minister, Pearson was the recipient of the Nobel Peace Prize in 1957, for his work establishing the United Nations Emergency Force and resolving the Suez Canal Crisis. As prime minister of Canada, his government introduced universal health care and adopted the nation's maple leaf flag and its national anthem.

Pierre Elliott Trudeau (1919–2000)

Terms: 1968–79; 1980–84
Birthplace: Montreal, Quebec
Political party: Liberal

Did you know? Pierre Trudeau was such a charismatic leader that the term "Trudeaumania" was coined during his time in office. While Prime Minister, Trudeau instituted the Canada Health Act, the Canadian Charter of Rights and Freedoms, and the Constitution Act 1982. Trudeau appointed the first woman speaker of the Senate, Muriel McQueen Fergusson, in 1972 and the first woman Governor General, Jeanne Sauvé, in 1984.

Charles Joseph ("Joe") Clark (1939–)
Term: 1979–80
Birthplace: High River, Alberta
Political party: Progressive Conservative Party

Did you know? Canada's youngest prime minister, Clark was elected at the age of 38 years old.

John Napier Turner (1929–)
Term: 1984
Birthplace: Richmond, Surrey, England
Political party: Liberal Party

Did you know? Turner became prime minister when Pierre Trudeau resigned from office in 1984. Turner immediately called a snap election in which his party lost. He served for 79 days as prime minister, the second-shortest tenure of all the nation's leaders.

(Martin) Brian Mulroney (1939–)
Term: 1984–93
Birthplace: Baie-Comeau, Quebec
Political party: Progressive Conservative Party

Did you know? In 1988, Brian Mulroney developed the Canadian Multiculturalism Act, which recognized multiculturalism as vital to the country and its future.

Guiding Canada
Prime Ministers

(A.) Kim Campbell, (1947–)

Term: 1993
Birthplace: Port Alberni, British Columbia
Political party: Progressive Conservative Party

Did you know? Campbell won the Progressive
Conservative leadership race that was held to replace
Prime Minister Brian Mulroney, who was set to retire
from politics amid flagging national support. Before
becoming prime minister, Campbell was appointed
justice minister in 1990.

Jean Chrétien (1934–)

Term: 1993–2003
Birthplace: Shawinigan, Quebec
Political party: Liberal Party

Did you know? Before serving as prime minister, Chrétien served as a cabinet member for six
prime ministers. During his long career in politics he also helped to create 10 national parks.
As prime minister he saw the nation through the
1995 Quebec referendum.

Paul Edgar Philippe Martin (1938–)

Term: 2003–06
Birthplace: Windsor, Ontario
Political party: Liberal Party

Did you know? Martin's accomplishments are
many, but he is most credited with delivering five
consecutive balanced budgets as finance minister
of Canada.

Stephen Harper (1959–)

Term: 2006–2015
Birthplace: Toronto, Ontario
Political parties: Progressive Conservative (1980s), Reform Party (1987), Canadian Alliance (2000), Conservative Party of Canada (2003)

Did you know? The nation's 22nd prime minister co-founded the Conservative Party of Canada.

Justin Pierre James Trudeau (1971–)

Term: 2015–
Birthplace: Ottawa, Ontario
Political party: Liberal Party of Canada

Did you know? The country's 23rd prime minister triggered a second "Trudeaumania" when he was elected on October 19, 2015. The eldest son of Pierre Elliott Trudeau, the country's 15th prime minister, is the first child of a past prime minister to be elected to office. Besides also possibly being the first prime minister with a tattoo, he is also the only prime minister born in Ottawa, the nation's capital.

14

▶ *British Columbia*
Community

The name of the present-day province of British Columbia is thought to have come from Queen Victoria and was introduced in 1858. The southern part of the colony had around that time been known to some as Columbia, after the river in the region, which had been named after the ship of American captain Robert Gray.

Largest living roof

The 2 ha "living roof" on the West Building of the Vancouver Convention Centre is the largest of its kind in Canada, and the largest non-industrial such roof in North America. Landscaped with more than 400,000 indigenous plants and grasses, the living roof helps insulate the building, keeping it cool in the summer and maintaining heat in the winter.

Longest history

The longest continuously occupied settlement in Canada is found on British Columbia's Haida Gwaii. It is estimated that an archeological site at Namu was inhabited around 10,000 years ago. Stone tools and remains of large butchered animals have been found at the site.

First gas station

Here's a fill 'er up first: the nation's first gas station opened in Vancouver in June 1907. Prior to the development of specialized gas stations, drivers had to fill up at distribution sites, which were typically located on the edges of towns or cities.

Highest dam

The highest dam in Canada is the Mica Dam in British Columbia, in operation since 1977. Located on the Columbia River, about 135 km from Revelstoke, the dam at the Mica Generating Station is 243 m high. The power plant accounts for 15 percent of the province's hydroelectric capacity.

First marine police

The Vancouver Police Department established the nation's first marine squad in 1911.

▶▶ *British Columbia*
Business/Industry

First aquarium
Vancouver Aquarium, located in the city's Stanley Park, was the country's first. When it opened on June 15, 1956, the aquarium was an 830 m² facility. Today, it's more than 9,000 m².

First orca study
The Vancouver Aquarium (see First aquarium) was the first facility in the world to study an orca. The aquarium acquired killer whale Moby Doll, a young male, in July 1969.

Busiest port

Port of Vancouver is the nation's largest and busiest port. More than 144 million tonnes of cargo moved through the port in 2019, with more than 3,000 foreign vessels arriving at the port.

First McDonald's restaurant

"Look for the Golden Arches!" The first McDonald's restaurant to operate outside of the United States opened in 1967 in Richmond, British Columbia. Over 50 years ago, the fast-food restaurant with the iconic golden arches opened on No. 3 Road and Granville Avenue, where it still stands today. Though the building has been completely remodelled, the arches have since been designated a heritage sign.

Most lumber

Not only does Canada lead the world as an exporter of softwood lumber, but British Columbia is the global export leader of the product. The province moves out more than 13 million cubic m of softwood, worth close to $2.9 billion. The United States, China and Japan are the three largest importers of the wood.

First shopping mall

Attention shoppers: Park Royal Shopping Centre in Vancouver is considered Canada's first shopping mall. It opened in September 1950.

►► *British Columbia*
People/Places/Things

Heli-skiing
Heli-skiing, in which a helicopter takes skiers to far-flung mountain runs, was invented in Canada in 1965. Hans Gmoser, who'd come to Canada from Austria in 1951, pioneered the concept in British Columbia's Bugaboo Mountains, where he built a lodge that still operates as a heli-skiing operation today.

Bathtub racing

Rub a dub dub — go! Nanaimo, British Columbia, held its first bathtub boat race in 1967, and the Nanaimo to Vancouver Great International World Championship race was born. "Tubbers" complete a one-mile race off Kits Beach near the Nanaimo Harbour. Despite carrying bathtubs, these boats can still reach speeds over 30 km per hour. The race was designed to shine a spotlight on the province, and it has achieved that and more, as bathtub races are now held in Auckland, New Zealand, and Bremerton, Washington.

Highest restaurant

Talk about dining at the height of style. Eagle's Eye restaurant at the Kicking Horse Mountain Resort near Golden, British Columbia, is the country's highest eatery. Located at the summit of the Golden Eagle Express gondola, it's 2,350 m above sea level. Reservations are highly recommended.

Lowest road

The lowest point on a public road in Canada is in the George Massey Tunnel under the Fraser River near Vancouver International Airport (it's 20 m below sea level). The 629 m tunnel, which opened in 1959, was considered an engineering marvel. It was the first project in North America to use immersed-tube technology. Six concrete segments, each 105 m long and weighing 16,783 tonnes, were built on dry land, joined, sealed and sunk into place.

First protected area for grizzly bears

British Columbia's Khutzeymateen Provincial Park was the first area in the country specifically protected for grizzly bears. Established in 1994, and also known as the Khutzeymateen/K'tzim-a-deen Grizzly Sanctuary, or "Valley of the Grizzly," the 43,000-ha park is located 45 km northeast of Prince Rupert and is home to about 50 grizzlies — one of the largest populations of the species in the province.

People/Places/Things

Longest peak-to-peak gondola

Sit back and enjoy the spectacular view while riding the Peak 2 Peak gondola lift that ferries skiers back and forth for 3 km between Whistler Mountain and Blackcomb Mountain. It is the highest cable car lift in the world, ascending 436 m above rivers, lakes, mountain peaks, glaciers and rugged terrain. Until 2017, it was recognized by Guinness World Records as the longest unsupported span between two cable car towers. Talk about a room with a view!

Terry Fox

British Columbian Terry Fox ran his Marathon of Hope from St. John's in Newfoundland and Labrador to Thunder Bay in Ontario. Fox died in 1981, but not before realizing his dream of raising one dollar for every person in Canada. His legacy continues with fund-raising events in his name.

First wheelchair around the world

Man in Motion, no doubt. Canadian Rick Hansen, born on August 26, 1957, in Port Alberni, British Columbia, became world famous in 1985 when he travelled more than 40,000 km around the world through 34 countries in his wheelchair to raise awareness for spinal cord injuries and research. Dubbed the Man in Motion World Tour, Hansen's feat — the first such ever — raised more than $26 million.

Ogopogo

Canada has its very own Loch Ness monster, which is said to roam British Columbia's Lake Okanagan. Every year, dozens of Canadians report sightings of the elusive Ogopogo (or N'ha-a-itk, "water demon," in Salish). The 40- to 50-foot-long sea serpent has been cited in Canadian folklore dating back to the 1700s. Though it may be the stuff of legends, the sea serpent remains a part of British Columbia's heritage today — even gracing the province's postal stamp during the 1990s. Scientists believe the legendary snake-like creature is more likely a form of primitive whale, Basilosaurus cetoides, which lived 35 to 40 million years ago. If this is the case, it begs the question how is it that many people have caught a glimpse of this creature in the last few years, with the most recent sighting having been in 2019?

15

Alberta | **Community**

The province of Alberta was named by the Marquess of Lorne, the Governor General of Canada between 1878 and 1883, after his wife, Princess Louise Caroline Alberta, the daughter of Queen Victoria.

Highest big city

At an elevation of 1,048 m, Calgary is Canada's highest big city.

Fastest growth

Alberta is growing by leaps and bounds, and it isn't just Calgary (pictured here), which has long held a top spot on the list of the nation's fastest-growing major cities (it was No. 1 in 2010 and No. 2 in 2019). Of all cities in the country, Alberta boasts five of the top-10 spots on the nation's growth list. And in 2019 Edmonton took the crown for the fastest-growing major city in Canada.

Greenest city

It's nicknamed "Festival City" owing to its year-round slate of cultural events, but an equally apt moniker for Edmonton might be "City of Green." Alberta's capital lays claim to one of the largest urban green spaces in North America. "The Ribbon of Green" winds its way through the city along the shores of the North Saskatchewan River, with nature areas and more than 150 km of trails.

Largest military training area

Canadian Forces Base Suffield, north of Medicine Hat, Alberta, is the nation's largest military training area in Canada. The base, which falls under the command of the 3rd Canadian Division, covers 2,690 km².

First Canadian mosque

The Al Rashid Mosque in Edmonton, Alberta, was the first Muslim mosque in Canada. It opened on December 12, 1938. The mosque was designated a historic building and moved to Fort Edmonton Park.

Largest pedestrian skywalk pathway

Calgary's +15 Skyway is a system of elevated pedestrian walkways (including a series of enclosed bridges) that connect buildings in the city's downtown core. It is the largest network of its kind on Earth. Called the "+15" because it's about 15 feet above the ground, the 18 km system now has 62 bridges.

Business/Industry

Best ski resort

If you're looking for a ski run, look no further than Alberta's Lake Louise Ski Resort, the nation's best in 2019, as voted by the World Ski Awards. In fact, the 145-run resort has snagged the top honour seven of the eight years the prize has been awarded!

Highest wages

Want to make some serious salary? Alberta's the place to be for that. In 2017 Statistics Canada ranked five Albertan communities among the top 10 in average full-time hourly wages, with Wood Buffalo–Cold Lake, Alberta, coming in with the top average hourly wage at $34.35.

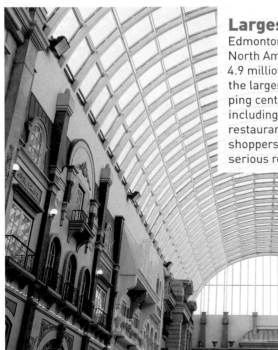

Who's got the beef?

Alberta, that's who! Alberta's beef farmers are a proud lot, and they should be. Alberta is home to nearly five million beef cattle, which accounts for more than 41 percent of Canada's herd!

World's only ammolite producer

The rainbow-coloured gem ammolite is one of the newest mined gemstones and one of the rarest. Found only in North America's Rocky Mountains, the gem is currently only mined in St. Mary River, Alberta, which is where the Korite mine, the largest ammolite mine in the world, is also located. The mine has produced over 42 million carats of the gemstone since its opening in 2003.

Largest shopping mall

Edmonton is home to the largest mall in North America, the West Edmonton Mall, at 4.9 million m². From 1981 until 2004 it was the largest mall in the world. The shopping centre boasts 800 stores and services, including two hotels and more than 100 restaurants. Approximately 30.8 million shoppers descend on it each year. That's serious retail therapy.

▶▶ *Alberta*
People/Places/Things

First planetarium
Sit back and enjoy the view. Canada's first planetarium, the Queen Elizabeth II Planetarium in Edmonton, opened on September 22, 1960.

Largest living history museum
Want to get a load of history? Try a visit to Fort Edmonton Park, known alternatively as "Canada's largest living history museum" or "the largest historical theme park in Canada." Among the attractions at the 64 ha park: more than 80 historical buildings, a steam-engine train, four early-1900 streetcars and a stagecoach.

Greatest Outdoor Show on Earth
Every summer the Calgary Stampede closes the city's downtown core for one of the world's largest rodeos. Founded in 1912, this 10-day event features a parade, midway, stage shows, concerts, agricultural competitions, chuckwagon racing, barbecues, and various art exhibitions. With over a million spectators each year, it's no wonder the Calgary Stampede has joined the ranks of the Pro Rodeo Hall of Fame.

First international peace park

Except for that war we won in 1812, Canada and the United States have had a relatively cordial relationship. Indeed, in 1932, the nations joined to create the world's first international peace park, Waterton-Glacier International Peace Park. (There are now 170 peace parks around the globe.) Together, Alberta's Waterton Lakes National Park and Montana's Glacier National Park form this 4,556 km² cross-border park, which was designated a UNESCO World Heritage Site on December 6, 1995.

Best buffalo jump

Talk about a literal place name! Alberta's Head-Smashed-In Buffalo Jump is considered one of the Earth's oldest, largest and best-preserved buffalo jumps. Now a UNESCO World Heritage Site, the spot was used by Indigenous peoples for close to 6,000 years to drive plains bison to their deaths by stampeding them off the edge of the cliffs. They would collect the meat to eat and use the hide and bones for clothes and tools.

The most horse-drawn vehicles

The continent's largest collection of horse-drawn vehicles resides at the Remington Carriage Museum in Cardston, Alberta. The museum boasts more than 270 carriages, buggies, wagons and sleighs from the 19th and early 20th centuries.

First national park

Canada's first national park, Banff National Park, was created in 1885, and was the world's third national park. The 6,641 km² protected area is the most-visited national park in the country.

16

Saskatchewan
Community

The name Saskatchewan is derived from Cree *kisiskâciwanisîpiy*, meaning "swift-flowing river." Saskatchewan became a province of Canada on September 1, 1905.

One city, two provinces

Here's a unique geographical distinction: Lloydminster is the only city in Canada that straddles a provincial border. Located almost the same distance from both Edmonton and Saskatoon, Lloydminster was first settled in 1903. When the provinces of Alberta and Saskatchewan were formed in 1905, the settlement was split along the 4th meridian, the provincial boundary. On May 20, 1930, the two communities were reunited as a single municipality.

Art deco bridge

Albert Street Memorial Bridge claims to be the longest bridge over the shortest span of water in the world.

RCMP historic training site

All cadets of the Royal Canadian Mounted Police undergo their initial basic training at the RCMP Academy "Depot" Division in Regina. Established in 1885, the site was once the headquarters of the North-West Mounted Police and then later, the Royal North-West Mounted Police.

Largest geothermal mineral pool

Looking for natural relaxation? Try the Temple Gardens Mineral Spa Resort in Moose Jaw, Saskatchewan. It's home to the nation's largest therapeutic geothermal mineral water pool. The pool's waters are drawn from an ancient seabed more than 1,350 m underground and stay warm throughout the year.

Business/Industry

Largest mustard producer

If you like your mustard, thank Saskatchewan. The prairie province is the world's largest mustard exporter. In 2017, the province produced 94,500 tonnes of mustard in three different types — yellow, brown and oriental.

Largest fertilizer company

You could say it's a growing business. Nutrien, based in Saskatoon, Saskatchewan, is the world's largest fertilizer company by capacity. It produces fertilizers from potash, phosphate and nitrogen.

Leading flaxseed producer

Canada is among the world's largest producers of flaxseed, making 19.8 percent of the global supply. The grand majority of that comes from Saskatchewan. Oil from flaxseed is used to create a host of products such as cooking oil and paint; its meal is used to make animal feed; and its wheat fibres have been used to make linen. The prairie sky that covers the province, along with Saskatchewan's dry climate, creates the perfect conditions in which this crop can grow.

Largest uranium mine

Saskatchewan's McArthur River mine is the largest high-grade uranium mine on Earth. It can produce more than 8.16 million kg of uranium each year.

Spacey tech

Located in Saskatoon, SED Systems is a world-class communications company specializing in satellite communications, including being the 24/7 watchdog of Canada's newest Earth observation satellites, known as the RADARSAT Constellation (seen here housed in a rocket before launch in 2019).

▶▶ *Saskatchewan*
People/Places/Things

Highest sports merchandise sales

Football is not just a sport in Saskatchewan; it's a way of life — which is why it's no surprise that the Saskatchewan Roughriders are the third-highest-selling merchandise out of all of the country's sports teams.

Longest-running historical theatre production

The Trial of Louis Riel is the longest-running historical theatre production in North America. Performed in Regina, Saskatchewan, the play was written in 1967 by John Coulter as a project to commemorate Canada's centennial. The play is now in its 53rd year of production and has become a staple at the Royal Saskatchewan Museum.

RIEL

Tommy Douglas (1904–1986)

T.C. (Tommy) Douglas, born in Falkirk, Scotland, in 1904, is considered the father of socialized medicine in Canada. During the Great Depression, Douglas and his wife and children moved to Weyburn, Saskatchewan, where he would soon enter politics and the fight for all Canadians to have access to medical care. Douglas eventually led the Co-operative Commonwealth Federation to power in Saskatchewan, becoming premier of the province in 1944. In the 17 years he was in office, Douglas introduced several government programs, including the Saskatchewan Bill of Rights and a universal health-insurance system, both of which were eventually adopted across the nation.

Largest capital building

The prairie vistas are not the only big things in Saskatchewan. The province's legislative building in Regina is the largest capital building in Canada. Planning for the building began less than a year after Saskatchewan became a province on September 1, 1905. The home of Saskatchewan's legislative assembly, the building opened on October 12, 1912, and is surrounded by one of the largest urban parks in North America. The façade and interior reflect the beaux-arts architectural style of the time.

Most road

If someone tells you to hit the road in Saskatchewan, be prepared for a very long walk. The province has more road surface than any other in the country: a total of 250,000 km.

17

Manitoba | **Community**

It's believed there are two principal origins for the name of the province of Manitoba. The more likely inspiration for the name is from the Cree word *manitowapow*, or "the strait of the spirit, or manitobau." This comes from the loud sound made by pebbles on Manitoba Island in Lake Manitoba. The second possible origin is from the Assiniboine words *mini* and *tobow*, which combined mean "lake of the prairie."

Canada 8

postes postage

Nellie McClung 1873–1951

First province where women could vote

Manitoba was the first province in Canada to grant women the right to vote, in 1916. First proposed by Manitoba's Icelandic community in the 1870s, the fight for women's suffrage was taken up by a team of women, including Dr. Mary Craw- ford, Lillian Beynon Thomas and Nellie McClung.

Most Icelanders

Given its reputation as being particularly cold (temperature-wise), is it any wonder that Manitoba is home to the largest Icelandic population outside of Iceland? Between 1870 and 1915, 20,000 Iceland- ers immigrated to the province — nearly a quarter of Iceland's population at the time. Today Manitoba's provincial government continues to appeal to Iceland- ers to settle there.

Polar bear capital of the world

Churchill, Manitoba, is world renowned as the polar bear capital of the world, thanks largely to its accessibility to the polar bear habitat. The bears can be seen through the summer, starting after mid-July, but it's not until October that the white bear's numbers really build. Through October and early November, it's possible to see 40 or more bears a day. The town sees so many polar bears that it opened its very own polar bear prison in 1981. The Polar Bear Holding Facility is housed in what used to be a military aircraft hangar. The facility has 28 cells, where the bears are held for 30 days before being transported by helicopter to the sea ice. Talk about catch and release!

Most preserved historic downtown

Winnipeg's Exchange District, a national historic site, is considered one of the best preserved and largest collections of terra cotta and cutstone architecture in North America. The 20-block area, the original core of Winnipeg, boasts about 150 heritage buildings, including early skyscrapers.

►► *Manitoba*
Business/Industry

Most Inuit art

Established in 1912, the Winnipeg Art Gallery claims a couple of Canadian superlatives. It's home to the world's largest public collection of contemporary Inuit art, with more than 13,000 works. The gallery also offers the largest program of art classes in the country, with professional artists teaching classes for children and adults.

Canola

Its name kind of gives it away. Canola, the globe's only invented-in-Canada oilseed crop, was created in the 1970s by researchers from Agriculture and Agri-Food Canada and the University of Manitoba. Today, canola is considered one of the most important oilseed crops in the world and has proved to be the most lucrative for Canadian farmers.

Slurpee capital of the world

Winnipeg is famous for many things, but did you know it's considered the Slurpee capital of the world? The crown is based on having the highest average number of Slurpee cups sold per store each year (400,000). The 7-Eleven store on Portage Avenue sells the second-most Slurpees in the country.

Only Arctic deep-water port

The Port of Churchill is Canada's only arctic deep-water port for shipping grain and other cargo across the world. As the sea route to the port is only passable from July to November, the port was closed in 2016. It reopened in 2019 and is expected to be the beginning of the Artic Bridge, a sea route that will allow for goods to be shipped between Murmansk, Russia, and Churchill, Manitoba.

Human-rights dedicated museum

Winnipeg is also home to the Canadian Museum for Human Rights. Opened on September 20, 2014, it is the only museum in the world that is solely dedicated to human rights issues and education.

People/Places/Things

Most outdoor musicals

The Rainbow Stage in Kildonan Park in Winnipeg is Canada's largest and longest-running outdoor theatre. Since its opening in 1953, the theatre has show-cased 140 productions.

Colder than Mars

In 2013, Winnipeggers experienced a deep freeze that saw temperatures drop within the province to levels colder than that of Mars. It seems NASA noticed, too, as two years later they named a small area of Mars "Winnipeg."

WINNIE-THE-BEAR

ON AUGUST 24TH 1914, WHILE ENROUTE OVERSEAS DURING WORLD WAR I LIEUTENANT HARRY COLEBOURN, V.S. OF THE 34TH FORT GARRY HORSE REGIMENT OF MANITOBA PURCHASED A BLACK CANADIAN BEAR CUB AT WHITE RIVER, ONTARIO. HE NAMED HER WINNIE AFTER WINNIPEG HIS HOME TOWN. THE BEAR BECAME THE PET OF THE SOLDIERS. WHILE LIEUTENANT COLEBOURN SERVED IN FRANCE, SHE WAS LEFT IN THE CARE OF THE LONDON ZOO IN 1919 HE GAVE HER TO THE ZOO WHERE SHE WAS VISITED AND LOVED BY MANY, INCLUDING THE AUTHOR A. A. MILNE AND HIS SON CHRISTOPHER.

IN 1926, A.A. MILNE GAVE THE FICTIONAL CHARACTER WINNIE-THE-POOH NAMED AFTER LIEUTENANT COLEBOURN'S BEAR, TO CHRISTOPHER ROBIN AND HIS FRIENDS FOR POSTERITY. WINNIE DIED AT THE LONDON ZOO ON MAY 12, 1934.

"WINNIE-THE-BEAR", BY SCULPTOR WILLIAM EPP, WAS DEDICATED TO THE CHILDREN OF THE WORLD ON AUGUST 6, 1992.

Snow road

Winter driving here is recommended. The Wapusk Trail road is the longest seasonal winter road in the world, according to Guinness World Records. The 752 km road is constructed annually in January between Gillam, Manitoba, and Peawanuck, Ontario, on snow and ice.

Inspiration for Winnie the Pooh

The iconic teddy bear was inspired by a real-life black bear cub named Winnie that was named after Winnipeg, the capital city of Manitoba.

The name Ontario is likely derived from Amerindian and was first applied to the Great Lake bearing the same name. It may come from *onitariio*, which means "beautiful lake," or *kanadario*, meaning "sparkling or beautiful water." Europeans eventually began using the name to refer to the land along the lake, and over time to increasingly larger areas north of the lake.

Most cars

When it comes to cars, there's a good chance it comes from Ontario. The province is one of the world's top 10 producers of light vehicles, with Canadian plants churning out more than two million vehicles each year for brands like Chrysler, Dodge, Ford, GM, Lincoln, Honda, Toyota and Lexus.

First computerized traffic control

Toronto was the first city in the world with a computerized traffic control system. In 1963, the city implemented the system to automate traffic signals. It required a 4.5-tonne air conditioning unit to keep it cool. Essentially, it was a clock that used predetermined plans to regulate traffic patterns during different parts of the day.

First traffic lights

The first traffic lights in Canada went up on June 11, 1925, at the intersection of Main and King streets in east Hamilton. The traffic light, which was made in the United States, proved problematic, as it had been designed for use at right-angle intersections, while Main and King crisscross at an angle. As a result, drivers were sometimes confused as to which light was meant for them. Another problem? Local residents weren't fond of the loud bell that accompanied the amber light.

Largest transit system

The Toronto Transit Commission, or TTC, is the largest public transit system in Canada and the third largest in North America. More than 520 million passengers use the system annually, and in 2019 the TTC welcomed the system's 32 billionth rider since opening in 1954.

Most immigrants

There's no doubt that Toronto is Canada's most multicultural city. The Greater Toronto Area is home to the largest percentage of immigrants in the country, with 35 percent of the nation's foreign-born residents. More than 2.7 million immigrants call Toronto home, making up 46 percent of the city's population. The largest percentage of the newcomers to the GTA are from India, at 11.9 percent, followed by China, with 9.9 percent of the immigrant population.

Most multicultural city

Talk about your united nations. Toronto is considered by many to be the most multicultural city in the world. More than 100 languages and dialects are spoken there.

First subway

A better way? The city of Toronto unveiled the nation's first subway system on March 31, 1954. The first line ran largely beneath Yonge Street. It encompassed 12 stops, from Union Station on Front Street at the south end to Eglinton Avenue at the north. Today the system boasts 75 stations and 169 conventional bus and streetcar routes.

Busiest highway

If you regularly drive along Highway 401 through Toronto, this may come as little surprise — and may be dismally deflating: the stretch is the busiest highway on the continent. It's estimated that an average of more than 425,000 vehicles travel the route daily, and some days the traffic surpasses half a million vehicles.

Largest entertainment venue

Toronto's Exhibition Place is the nation's largest entertainment venue. The 77 ha site is home to a variety of exhibition buildings, conference facilities and sporting venues, such as the Enercare Centre, the Better Living Centre, Ricoh Coliseum and BMO Field. It attracts more than 5.5 million visitors each year. Exhibition Place also hosts big events, including the Canadian National Exhibition and the Royal Winter Fair.

Most hockey

The Greater Toronto Hockey League boasts the most minor hockey players in Canada, annually averaging nearly 40,000 players, it is the largest youth hockey organization in the world!

Painted road lines

Sometimes you just have to draw a line. Indeed, in the 1930s, engineer John D. Millar of the Ontario Department of Transport came up with the idea of painting lines on roads to ensure traffic stayed in its own lane. The world's first road lines were painted on a stretch of highway near the Ontario–Quebec border, and within three years the lines were commonplace throughout the continent.

▶▶ *Ontario*
Business/Industry

Largest underground shopping centre

You could call it the walkway to retail heaven. The PATH system in Toronto, an underground pathway that links 30 km of shops under a large portion of the city's downtown core, is considered the largest underground shopping complex in the world. PATH boasts 371,600 m² of retail space, houses about 1,200 shops and services, and connects more than 75 buildings.

Largest youth employer

Help wanted. Canada's Wonderland, the nation's largest amusement park, located just north of Toronto, is the largest single-location employer of youth in Canada. It's also the top employer in York Region, the municipality where it's located. The park employs more than 4,000 seasonal staff.

Richest vein of silver

The world's richest vein of silver was found in Cobalt, Ontario, in 1903. In the following 60 years, silver mines in the area produced a total of almost 1.2 million tonnes of silver ore and concentrates, and the total production over that time was more than 11,921 million grams of silver. The silver rush ended somewhat abruptly in the mid-20th century, and the town turned its mining attention to the mineral it was named after. Thanks to improved technology, cobalt had become more useful.

Largest grain capacity

Ontario's Port of Thunder Bay has the largest grain storage capacity in North America. The port's eight terminals have a capacity of 1.2 million tonnes.

Largest mining province

When it comes to mining in Canada, images of the Yukon gold rush come to mind. Ontario, however, is the country's leading mining province, contributing more than 21 percent of the nation's mining value. Ontario leads the way in the nation's production of gold, nickel, sand and gravel, and stone. It is also the second-leading producer of copper.

Largest stock exchange/TSE firsts

The Toronto Stock Exchange is the largest stock exchange in Canada, the third largest in North America and the eighth largest in the world. It opened on October 25, 1861, and 18 stocks could be traded. The TSE became a publically traded company in 2000 (two years later adopting the abbreviation TSX). In 2008 it acquired the Montreal Exchange.

Business/Industry

Most wind power

Boasting more than 2,681 wind turbines with a capacity of more than 5,436 megawatts (enough to power almost one million homes), Ontario is the nation's leader in wind-power production.

Largest chocolate seller

Laura Secord, the chocolate company formed in 1913, is the nation's largest chocolatier. Today the company boasts more than 100 stores across the country and more than 400 products.

First milk pasteurization

The Hospital for Sick Children installed the first milk pasteurization plant in Canada in 1908 — 30 years before the process was mandatory.

First oil company

Oil! The first oil company in North America was founded in the aptly named community of Oil Springs, Ontario, southeast of Sarnia. On December 18, 1854, Charles Tripp received approval for his commercial oilwell.

Largest convention centre

Looking for a place to show off? Try Toronto's Direct Enercare Centre, the nation's largest convention and exhibition facility. Located at Exhibition Place, on the west side of the city's downtown, the centre boasts 99,592,000 m² of exhibit space in eight halls, plus the Ricoh Coliseum, an 8,200-seat arena.

Largest solar farms

The Grand Renewable Solar Project (Haldimand County) and the Sol-Luce Kingston project are two of North America's largest solar farms, each with a total capacity of 100 megawatts of energy — each capable of powering 17,000 homes.

▶▶ *Ontario*
People/Places/Things

Largest indoor aquarium

Ripley's Aquarium of Canada in Toronto is the nation's largest indoor aquarium. The 12,500 m² attraction, which opened on October 16, 2013, boasts more than 16,000 marine animals and more than 450 species.

Largest art school

The Ontario College of Art & Design University, located in Toronto, is the nation's largest art school. Founded in 1876 as the Ontario School of Art, OCAD now hosts some 4,346 undergraduates. In an average year the university is attended by students from more than 50 different countries.

First drive-in

The nation's first drive-in theatre opened in Stoney Creek, Ontario, in 1946. The Skyway Drive-In had a 705-car capacity.

First retractable roof

Toronto's Rogers Centre boasted the world's first fully retractable roof when the building opened in June 1989 (at the time it was called SkyDome). The 11,000-tonne roof is made of four sections and opens (and closes) in a semicircular motion in 20 minutes. The current home of Major League Baseball's Toronto Blue Jays, the stadium also hosts numerous other sporting and entertainment events. Indeed, more than 60 million people have passed through the building's turnstiles.

People/Places/Things

First museum

The first museum in Canada, and the country's oldest, is that of Thomas Barnett, an English "collector" who immigrated to Canada in the early 1820s. He opened a museum of his personal collection of local and foreign artifacts in Niagara Falls in 1827. That museum became today's Niagara Falls Museum.

Largest sports complex

Whitby, Ontario, located about an hour east of Toronto, is the home of the country's largest municipally owned and operated multi-use sports complex. The Iroquois Park Sports Centre houses six arenas, two swimming pools, six tennis courts, one baseball diamond and two softball diamonds, one soccer field, and a strength and conditioning training facility. It is surrounded by 50 ha of parkland.

Craig and Marc Kielburger (1982–; 1977–)

In 1995, Craig and Marc Kielburger founded We Charity (formerly Free the Children), the world's largest youth-driven charity.

Largest children's hospital

If buildings had a heart, this one's would be pretty big. Toronto's Hospital for Sick Children, known as SickKids, is the country' largest facility dedicated to children's health. The hospital's history dates back to 1875, and today about 15,000 youngsters stay at the facility each year, while another nearly 300,000 visit the hospital's more than 100 clinics annually.

Largest university

Talk about student life! The University of Toronto is the country's largest university, with enough students to create a small city — more than 91,000 students at three campuses (St. George, Mississauga and Scarborough). U of T offers more than 700 undergraduate programs and 300 graduate programs. Its operations budget for 2018–19 was $2.7 billion.

19

Quebec
Community

The name of the province of Quebec almost certainly comes from First Nations languages, specifically and most likely Algonquin. The name was first applied to the province's current capital in various spellings (Quebecq, Kébec, Quebec) in the 17th century, and is a reference to the Algonquin word for "narrow passage" or "strait," in reference to the narrowing of the St. Lawrence River in the area. The same word is also common to Cree and Mi'Kmaq.

Only walled city

Did you know that Quebec City is the only walled city in North America and the oldest city on the continent north of the Mexico border? It was founded in 1608. The Historic District of Old Quebec is a UNESCO world heritage site, the first city in North America to receive the designation.

Busiest subway

The Montreal Metro is the nation's busiest subway system. More than a million passengers travel through the system's 68 stations daily.

First hospital

Quebec City's Hôtel-Dieu was the first hospital in America north of Mexico. It was founded by three Augustinian nuns in 1639.

First public hospital

John Molson, founder of the brewing company, was instrumental in the establishment of Montreal's first public hospital, Montreal General Hospital. It opened on May 1, 1819.

First electric streetlights

Quebec City's Dufferin Terrace was the first area in Canada to have electrical street-lights. The lights debuted in 1883, just three years after the first test of outdoor electrical lighting in North America.

First YMCA

The first YMCA in North America started in Montreal on November 25, 1851. When it began, the Y had strong ties to Protestant churches, but this soon changed as people from all religions were welcomed. The YMCA of Greater Montreal went on to open the first public library in the city in 1854.

Busiest bridge

The busiest crossing in Canada just got a whole lot busier. On June 24, 2019, the first motorists made their way across the new Samuel De Champlain Bridge, the sleek and modern replacement for the crumbling Champlain Bridge (the green steel bridge at the right in the photo). Providing passage over the St. Lawrence River from the island of Montreal to the south shore, the new bridge (complete with expanded auto lanes and dedicated lanes for light rail and pedestrians) will certainly move more than its predecessor's impressive 60 million vehicles per year.

▶▶ *Quebec*
Business/Industry

Largest milk production

Got milk? Quebec is the nation's largest milk producer, with the province producing three billion litres of milk per year. It also has the most organic milk producers, at 136.

Largest cheese producer

And not by a little bit, either. Quebec's share of Canada's cheese production is a whopping 50 percent! From multinationals to small artisanal producers, the province boasts 500 different kinds of cow's milk cheese.

Most maple syrup

Did you know that Canada has a reserve of maple syrup in case of a worldwide shortage? That's because Canada is the world's leading producer of maple syrup (the United States is the only other country to produce it). Canada produces 82 percent of the globe's maple syrup, which is valued at more than $177 million. More than 90 percent of Canadian maple syrup comes from Quebec. About 83 percent of the syrup produced in Canada is exported.

Largest log cabin

Where else in the world would you find the globe's largest log cabin but in Canada? Specifically, in Montebello, Quebec. Built in 1930 from 10,000 western red cedar logs and used as a private fishing lodge, the 211-room building is now the Fairmont Le Château Montebello.

Business/Industry

Most choppers

Bell Helicopter, owned by Textron Inc. out of Texas, produces the majority of the world's commercial helicopters. Since 1986, the majority of the company's commercial helicopter assembly has been based in Mirabel, Québec, where choppers like the Bell Boeing 505 Jet Ranger X (pictured here) are made.

Commercial jet maker

Created in Quebec by Bombardier, the A220 (formerly known as the C series) is an energy-efficient commercial aircraft. Although Bombardier sold the C series to Airbus of France, the plane is still manufactured in the province in a factory just north of Montreal.

Canada's sky leader

No province contributes more to the $13 billion aerospace sector than Quebec. From flight simulators to planes to helicopters, Quebec is responsible for 51 percent of all aerospace manufacturing in Canada and 23 percent of all maintenance and repair.

First commercial radio station

Canada's first commercial radio station (and some would argue, the world's first too) was XWA Montreal, subsequently known as CFCF, CIQC and AM 940. It hit the airwaves in 1919 and was live until its last broadcast in January 2010.

First daily newspaper

The *Montreal Daily Advertiser*, established in 1883, was the nation's first daily newspaper. It went bankrupt within a year of its first edition.

First bilingual daily newspaper

Canada's first bilingual newspaper, the *Quebec Gazette*, was based in Quebec City and was established in 1764 by two Philadelphia printers, William Brown and Thomas Gilmore.

Gaming capital

Did you know that Canada's second-biggest city, Montreal, is also the nation's largest producer of video games? Often referred to as the gaming capital of Canada, the city has become quite a powerhouse within the gaming industry. In fact, Montreal is the fifth-largest video game hub in the world, after Tokyo, Japan; London, England; San Francisco, California and Austin, Texas. Although 80 percent of all game studios in the country are located in Quebec, British Columbia and Ontario, Quebec is home to the lion's share — 29.4 percent.

First protected area

Montreal's Mount Royal Park is considered Canada's first protected area. It was inaugurated on Queen Victoria's birthday, May 24, in 1876.

First music and voice radio broadcast

Seems as though Canadian domination of the music charts dates back to 1906. That was the year Canadian inventor Reginald Fessenden, born in Knowlton, Quebec, made the first public broadcast of music and voice on December 24 from his headquarters in Brant Rock, Massachusetts. In the broadcast Fessenden included a Bible passage, a phonograph recording of Handel, and he played "O Holy Night" on the violin.

►► *Quebec*
People/Places/Things

First art gallery

Artist Joseph Légaré opened the first art gallery in Canada. The gallery, which featured his personal collection of art (his own and what he had collected), opened in 1833 in Quebec City. His painting, *The Fire in the Saint-Jean Quarter, Seen Looking Westward*, 1848, is seen here.

First movie theatre

Pass the popcorn. The first commercial movie theatre in North America opened on January 1, 1906, in Montreal. The Ouimetoscope was converted from a tavern to a 500-seat cinema with a small screen.

First performance of "O Canada"

"O Canada" was performed for the first time on June 24, 1880, in Quebec City. The music was composed by Calixa Lavallée and the first lyrics, in French, were written by Adolphe-Basile Routhier. The tune did not become the country's official national anthem until July 1, 1980.

Most totem poles

The Canadian Museum of History is home to the world's largest indoor collection of totem poles. Many of the museum's totem poles are housed in the building's dramatic Grand Hall.

20

Newfoundland and Labrador | **Community**

The name Newfoundland comes from England's King Henry VII, who referred to the island as "New Found Launde" by 1852. (Its French name, Terre Neuve, was used as early as 1510.)

Most colourful downtown

Once you reach downtown St. John's, you'll quickly realize why it's often referred to as "jellybean row." True to its nickname, its slanted streets are lined with rowhouses painted in vibrant shades from all spectrums of the rainbow. The province's fishing roots are also on display in Jellybean Row, as, historically, the homes were painted in vivid colours to guide sailors home to their families, as the colourful facades were a beacon welcoming them home before their ships reached port.

First city

St. John's, Newfoundland, is the most easterly city in North America. But it also claims to be the continent's oldest city. St. John's has long been a centre of fisheries in the New World — the earliest records of battles over control of the city's port date back to 1555.

First English colony

There are some great place names in Newfoundland and Labrador (Come By Chance and Heart's Content, for instance). Cupids is another. But the town on Conception Bay is significant for more than just its unique name. It was the first English colony in Canada and is also the oldest continuously occupied English settlement in the country. In 1610, English colonist John Guy established a plantation at what was then known as Cuper's Cove.

Best integrated walkway system

Care for a stroll? Well, if you're in Newfoundland, the Grand Concourse is the best place to start. The 120 km integrated walkway system links the communities of St. John's, Mount Pearl and Paradise through their major parks and waterways.

Most Irish place in the world outside of Ireland

Over 100 ships sailed from Ireland to Newfoundland in the late 1700s, ferrying thousands of people to a new beginning in Canada. The province's Irish roots are still evident today in places such as "the Irish loop," a rural part of the province where locals still speak in a thick Irish dialect, and particularly on Fogo Island, where Tilting residents proudly display flags celebrating their Irish heritage. It's no wonder Newfoundland is called the most Irish place in the world outside of Ireland.

Most varieties of spoken English

What did you say? Was that English? Newfoundlanders are known for their distinctive way of speaking. The province is home to more varieties of spoken English than anywhere else on Earth. The province's English dialects are so distinct that there's even a dictionary of Newfoundland English.

Business/Industry

World-class geological museum

Signal Hill, the site of the first-ever transatlantic wireless signal, is now the site of another world-class feature — the Johnson Geo Centre. The centre, opened in 1992, is dedicated to exploring the geological world found in Newfoundland and Labrador, including various exhibits from the oil and gas exploration industry and the natural resources found within the province, space exploration, and even an exhibit dedicated to the *Titanic* disaster.

Largest offshore drilling

Located in Jeanne d'Arc Basin, 315 km east off the coast of St. John's, Newfoundland, the Hibernia oil platform stretches 80 m to the ocean floor, and it is Canada's largest offshore oil drilling platform. The oil platform was built in 1997, just 15 years after the tragic sinking of the SS *Ocean Ranger* off the coast of Newfoundland, where it was drilling in the Hibernia oil field, during a storm that brought winds of 190 km per hour and waves as high as 6 m. The Hibernia platform has already been tested — in November 2018, the platform experienced a storm that brought winds of 130 km per hour, the strongest in 30 years. The platform fared well through the storm, as it was designed as a special gravity-based structure that could withstand being hit by a one-million-tonne iceberg (estimated to occur every 500 years).

Cape Race

In 1904, Marconi installed the first wireless station at Cape Race, on the southeastern tip of the Avalon Peninsula in Newfoundland, and it was that station that received the first distress call from the the RMS *Titanic* on April 14, 1912, before the ship sank. Operator James Godwin received the SOS signal from the *Titanic*, and he immediately relayed the message to other ships within proximity, in the hopes that one would reach the ship before it sank. Unfortunately, only the SS *Carpathian* was able to reach the *Titanic* in time, saving 705 passengers.

Richest sea harvest

Considered one of the world's largest and richest resource areas, the Grand Banks off the southeast coast of Newfoundland have been plumbed for resources since at least the 1400s. The banks are actually a series of raised under-water plateaus ranging between 36.5 and 185 m deep. The relatively shallow water allows a range of marine and plant life to thrive. Fishermen from around the Atlantic harvest haddock, ocean perch, crabs, clams and scallops, as well as hundreds of other species from these waters.

Historic hill

Signal Hill has long been embedded in Canada's communications history. Before Marconi received the first telegraphic Morse code radio trans-mission on the hill in 1901, signalmen would keep watch on the ocean below from the hill, on the lookout for approaching ships. As a ship would near the coast, the signal-men would raise flags to alert the people waiting on the harbour below of the names of the ships heading to port.

Oldest European funeral mount

Newfoundland is home to the oldest known funeral mount on the continent, the burial site of a child that dates to approximately 7,500 years ago.

Largest storm petrel colony

The Witless Bay Ecological Reserve (see Largest puffin colony) is also home to the continent's largest colony of Leach's storm petrel, a small black seabird. The second-largest such colony in the world, it is home to more than 620,000 pairs that nest on the island each year.

Largest puffin colony

The largest colony of Atlantic puffins in North America is found in Newfoundland's Witless Bay Ecological Reserve. The reserve, made up of four islands — Gull, Green, Great and Pee Pee, sees more than 260,000 pairs of puffins nest there in late spring and summer. The puffin is Newfoundland and Labrador's official bird.

First non-stop transatlantic flight

An epic dare: In 1913, the *Daily Mail*, a United Kingdom daily paper, offered £10,000 ($1 million today) to the first person to fly non-stop across the Atlantic Ocean. It took six years for aviation technology to advance enough for anyone to even attempt this feat. On June 15, 1919, John Alcock and Arthur Brown arrived in Newfoundland determined to collect the prize. While many had tried and failed, it took Alcock and Brown 16 hours to fly their Vickers Vimy airplane across the Atlantic. After several mishaps along the way, such as losing radio capacity shortly after takeoff, navigating through heavy fog, and even losing control of the airplane momentarily, the duo managed to land the aircraft in a bog in Clifton, Ireland, cementing their place in history as pilots of the first non-stop trans-Atlantic flight.

Easternmost point (Canada)

The most easterly point in Canada and North America is Cape Spear, Newfoundland.

Easternmost point (North America)

The most easterly point of *continental* North America is Cape St. Charles, Labrador.

21

New Brunswick
Community

What is present-day New Brunswick was once considered part of Nova Scotia. During the American Revolution (1775–1783), people loyal to Britain (known as Loyalists) moved to the area and pushed to form a new province. New Brunswick was created on September 10, 1784, and the name was chosen in honour of King George III, a descendant of the House of Brunswick.

Highest tides
Sure, Canada's Bay of Fundy has the highest tides in the world, but did you know that at some times of year the difference between low and high tide can be taller than a three-storey building? Indeed, Fundy's tides can differ by up to 16.27 m. Part of the reason for Fundy's dramatic tides is the V-shape of the bay, which funnels water into less and less space, causing the water to rise.

Canada's Chocolate Town
Sweet town! The old Ganong chocolate factory in St. Stephen, New Brunswick, now houses a tribute to the town's roots in this sweet treat — the Chocolate Museum.

Only bilingual province
The nation's only officially bilingual province? New Brunswick, where about 33 percent of people speak French.

First city

The oldest incorporated city in Canada? None other than Saint John, New Brunswick (pictured as the backdrop to these pages). At the end of the 1776 American Revolution, 14,000 American supporters of the British established two settlements at the mouth of the Saint John River (one on each side; Parrtown on the east and Carleton on the west). In 1785, the two settlements merged to form Canada's first city. Saint John is also the only city on the world-famous Bay of Fundy.

Oldest continuously running museum

In Canada, the New Brunswick Museum is the oldest continually running provincial museum. The museum's roots extend as far back as 1842, when it was opened by Abraham Gesner. Since then, the museum has changed hands several times during its operation until 1942, when it became a fully funded provincial museum accessible to the people of New Brunswick.

Summer White House

Campobello Island, New Brunswick, was frequently visited by President Roosevelt, the 32nd president of the United States. Roosevelt was so fond of the area he once had a summer home on the island. The property on which the 34-room residence still stands is now Roosevelt Campobello International Park, established as a symbol of the friendship between the United States and Canada on Campobello Island.

▶▶ *New Brunswick*
Business/Industry

Most Tim Hortons

Many Canadians consider Tims a national treasure, but the restaurant chain is practically embedded in Moncton culture, and rightly so as there are more Tim Hortons per capita in greater Moncton than there are anywhere else in Canada. There's one Tims for every 4,720 residents!

First McFlurry

Ron McLellan created this much-loved treat at his McDonald's franchise in Bathurst, New Brunswick, in 1995. After 25 years, this dessert is offered at various McDonald's franchises across the globe, with each country offering its own unique flavour mixes: McFlurries in Canada usually come with candy; however, the UK uses Cadbury Crème Eggs, Japan mixes in green tea, Argentinians enjoy dulce de leche and chocolate, and Thailand offers patrons tiramisu mixed into their delectable treats.

Lobster capital of the world

It's hardly an officially designated title, but the town of Shediac, New Brunswick, lays claim to its being the lobster capital of the world. Shediac is home to lobster fishermen (naturally), processing plants, live tanks and the famous mid-July Lobster Festival.

Foghorn

Spend any amount of time in the Maritimes and you'll see a lot of fog. So is it any wonder the world's first steam-operated foghorn was invented in New Brunswick? In 1854, after first-hand experience with the Bay of Fundy fog, Robert Foulis invented the device. The first was installed on the province's Partridge Island in 1859. Nations around the globe subsequently adopted the use of the horn.

Most french fries

Get out the ketchup. And lots of it. McCain Foods, whose global headquarters is located in Florenceville-Bristol, New Brunswick, is the world's largest manufacturer of french fries. Indeed, one of every three french fries eaten on Earth is a McCain fry.

►► *New Brunswick*
People/Places/Things

Largest whirlpool

The largest natural whirlpool in the western hemisphere is located in the Western Passage of Passamaquoddy Bay in the Bay of Fundy, to the west of Deer Island, New Brunswick. Called "Old Sow," the whirlpool infrequently and unpredictably forms a funnel in the water.

World-famous hill

Care to defy gravity? Magnetic Hill in Moncton, New Brunswick, is famous for doing just that. Thousands of curious drivers head to the hill every year excited to experience the mysterious force that pulls cars uphill on a downhill slope, seemingly against gravity. If you're wondering how this is possible, it's because the slopes on Magnetic Hill that are visible aboveground appear to head downward, but what you don't see is underground, where the true landscape reveals that the hill actually sits on a horizontal level. Together, the differing terrains create an optical illusion of rolling uphill on a downhill slope. Magnetic Hill is one of hundreds of gravity hills that can be found throughout the world.

First female sea captain

A very Kool woman. Myrtle Kool (or Molly, as she was sometimes called), born in Alma, New Brunswick, in 1916, was North America's first female sea captain. When Kool was 21 years old, she attended Saint John's Merchant Marine School. She soon became a mate on her father's ship, the SS *Jean K. Kool*, achieved her master's certificate, making her the first female master mariner in Canada and the second in the world. Kool's father would eventually hand over the reins of his ship, making his daughter its captain — and the first female on the continent to hold this role. Over the course of her life at sea, Kool guided her ship and crew through three ship-wrecks and an engine fire. She sailed the sea up until her retirement in 1944.

First Miss Canada

At 19 years old, Winnifred Blair, from Saint John, New Brunswick, was the first Miss Canada crowned on February 10, 1923. The pageant resulted in protests from feminist groups across the country and was subsequently closed down the next year. Another Miss Canada pageant was introduced in 1946, and it ran until 1992. In 2008, the competition reopened with a focus on personality and attitude.

Canadian UK Prime Minister

A little-known fact: Andrew Bonar Law, born in Rexton, New Brunswick, in 1858, served as the prime minister of the UK from 1922 to 1923.

22

Prince Edward Island
Community

Modern-day Prince Edward Island had a couple of different names before it received its current name in 1798 in honour of Prince Edward, Duke of Kent, and the father of Queen Victoria. The island was first known as Île de Saint Jean in the 17th century, then as St. John's Island after it became British property in 1759.

Birthplace of confederation

Although Prince Edward Island did not join Canada until 1873, the province is still considered the birthplace of Canada. PEI hosted the Charlottetown Conference of 1864, which led to the formation of Canada in 1867.

Most densely populated

Despite being Canada's smallest province, Prince Edward Island is the nation's most densely populated. It's estimated there are 25.1 individuals per square km on the island.

Victoria Park

The property on which Victoria Park stands started out as possibly the biggest backyard in Canada. In 1789, Lieutenant-Governor Edmund Fanning set aside 100 acres of crown land so that the governor's house could be built on it. When Goverment House (now called Fanningbank) was actually built in 1834, the provincial government noted the need for more city park space, so only 10 acres was used for the residence and 40 acres was given to the city of Charlottetown for the site of Victoria Park.

First European flag in Canada

The first recorded European flag to fly in North America had the flag of England on one side and the winged-lion pennant of St. Mark of Venice on the opposite side. It flew on St. John's Island (present-day Prince Edward Island) on June 24, 1497, planted by the crew of John Cabot.

No cars allowed

Can you imagine banning cars? Prince Edward Island did it in 1908. The government instituted the prohibition because many islanders thought the automobile was too noisy and scared horses. In 1913, the restriction was reduced and driving was banned on Tuesdays, Fridays, Saturdays and Sundays. It wasn't until 1918 that the province rescinded the ban entirely.

Regulated walrus hunt

In September 1770, the government of St. John's Island (modern-day Prince Edward Island) regulated the sea cow (walrus) hunt as its first legislative act. The move was aimed to protect the species' population.

▶▶ *Prince Edward Island*
Business/Industry

"Spud Island"

Canada's smallest province is also the biggest producer of potatoes, bringing in the most cash receipts for the crop. In 2018, potato crops earned Prince Edward Island's economy more than $500 million. The province produces 25 percent of Canada's potatoes. The potato is so beloved by islanders and is such an important crop for the province, it even has its own museum. They don't call Prince Edward Island "Spud Island" for nothing!

Aerospace hub

Prince Edward Island has become a hub for the aerospace manufacturing and repair industry. In fact, the sector accounts for 20 percent of Canada's exports, adding over $400 million annually to Canada's economy.

Irish moss

Irish moss is used in numerous household foods and products, from salad dressing, ice cream, chocolate milk and other dairy products to toothpaste, shampoos, paints and insect repellant. This unique seaweed can be found on the shores of Prince Edward Island. Islanders started harvesting the sea plant in the 1930s, but by the 1970s, cultivation of Irish moss would grow into a multimillion-dollar industry. However, since then the industry has been in steep decline and efforts are now being made to protect the remaining moss and harvest it sustainably.

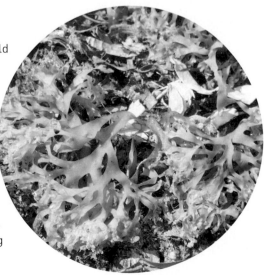

►► *Prince Edward Island*
People/Places/Things

Offical anthem

Prince Edward Island also has an official provincial anthem, which was adopted on May 7, 2010. "The Island Hymn" was written by novelist Lucy Maud Montgomery in 1908. The music was composed by Lawrence W. Watson. It also has a French version, "L'hymne de l'Île," that was adapted by Raymond J. Arsenault.

Fair Island of the sea,
We raise our song to thee,
The bright and blest;
Loyally now we stand
As brothers, hand in hand,
And sing God save the land
We love the best.

Mouse hunt

In 2010, Charlottetown sponsored a scavenger hunt that featured mice — though not the tiny, furry creatures usually scurrying through farmers' fields. Inspired by the children's book *The True Meaning of Crumbfest*, by Charlottetown author David Weale, the children used a list of clues that pointed the way to nine bronze statues of Eckhart the Mouse, the main character in Weale's story, hidden in various locations across the city.

Largest yard sale

Every year over 150 vendors shop their wares at Prince Edward Island's 70-Mile Yard Sale, which spans over 350 sites along the southeastern coast of the province. After 24 years, the yard sale continues to draw crowds of thousands of savvy shoppers.

Epic softball game

On June 30, 2008, two softball teams battled it out in Charlottetown for 96 hours! In the end, team Mark's Work Wearhouse bested team Hunter's Ale House 1066–874.

Bridge over icy waters

Opened on May 31, 1997, at a cost of $1 billion, the Confederation Bridge (linking Prince Edward Island and New Brunswick) is the largest bridge in the world that crosses ice-covered waters. Prince Edward Islanders voted to replace the ferry service connecting the island to the mainland with the curved 12.9 km bridge. In 1988, 59.4 percent of voters preferred the fixed link.

Singing sand

Though Basin Head Beach was named the top beach in Canada in 2013, what it is famous for is its singing sand. The sand that covers the beach has a high amount of silica and quartz, which squeaks underfoot when beach-goers walk along its shores, thus the term "singing sand."

The name Nova Scotia was first used to refer to the area of the modern-day province on September 29, 1621. Sir William Alexander was granted "the lands lying between New England and Newfoundland ... to be known as Nova Scotia, or "New Scotland.""

First social club

L'Ordre de Bon Temps ("The Order of Good Cheer") was North America's first social club. It was founded in 1606 in Port-Royal, Nova Scotia, by explorer Samuel de Champlain.

First Library

The first known private library collection in the Americas was at Port-Royal, Acadia (present-day Nova Scotia), and was established by Marc Lescarbot in 1606. Lescarbot, a lawyer and writer from France, participated in the first voyage of Samuel de Champlain and Pierre Du Gua de Monts to Acadia that year.

Welcome to Canada

Pier 21 is a national historic site that was once the gateway to Canada for one million immigrants between 1928 and 1971. It also served as the departure point for 368,000 Canadian military personnel during the Second World War. Currently the pier is the site of the Canadian Museum of Immigration.

A wee Scot

The island of Cape Breton is home to a thriving Scottish culture that includes a Gaelic College (the only institute of its kind in North America), and the most Gaelic speakers outside of Scotland. The island also hosts the Celtic Colours International Festival.

Longest downtown boardwalk

If you advance to this boardwalk, be prepared for a long walk. The Halifax Waterfront Boardwalk is one of the longest downtown boardwalks in the world. The 3.8 km trail runs from Pier 21 to Casino Nova Scotia and takes about 40 minutes to walk.

First lighthouse

It's no joke. The first documented lighthouse in Canada went into service on April 1, 1734, at Louisbourg, Nova Scotia. The stone tower was about 20 m tall and featured a fire chamber at the top fuelled by coal. It was destroyed by the British in 1758, and today a modern lighthouse sits on the same location.

First zoo

The first zoo in North America was opened by Andrew Downs in Halifax in 1847. Known as Downs' Zoological Gardens, the facility was home to the largest collection of birds, animals and plants outside England. The zoo's land and animals were eventually sold when in 1868 Downs was offered a job to set up a zoo in Central Park, New York City. Alas, for unknown reasons, the job didn't pan out and Downs returned to Halifax after three months.

First IKEA store

The first North American store of the Swedish furniture chain opened in Dartmouth, Nova Scotia, in 1977.

First naval dockyard

Built in 1759, the naval dockyard in Halifax was the first naval dockyard in North America.

Kerosene

Abraham Gesner of Cornwallis, Nova Scotia, is the inventor of kerosene. The geologist started experiments to distill oil in the form of kerosene in 1846 and had created the lamp oil by 1853. Around that time, the fuel became the lighting standard in homes. Thanks to his patents for distilling bituminuous materials, Gesner is also considered a founder of the modern petroleum industry.

First newspaper

It was a humble beginning, but an important one. Printed on half a foolscap sheet, Canada's first newspaper debuted on March 23, 1752. The day's edition of the *Halifax Gazette* boasted news from Europe, Britain and the other British colonies to the south.

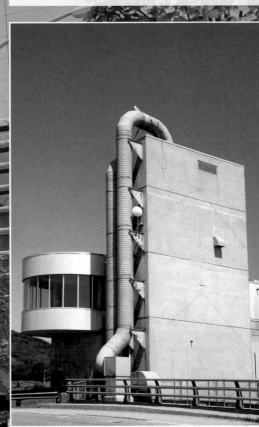

Fastest ship

The *Bluenose* fishing schooner first set sail on March 26, 1921. Captain Angus Walters and his crew depended on the vessel to get them back to port faster than their competitors in order to fetch the best price of the day for their catch, and the *Bluenose* always delivered. The *Bluenose* won its first International Fishermen's Race in October 1921 and lost only once in its 17-year racing career. The schooner is commemorated on the Canadian dime.

First tidal power plant

The first tidal power plant in the Americas, and the only one in North America, was built near Annapolis Royal, Nova Scotia, in 1984. The Annapolis Tidal Station has a capacity of 20 megawatts, and depending on the tides, a daily output of roughly 80 to 100 megawatt hours. It boasts the world's largest straight-flow turbine generator, capable of producing more than 30 million kilowatt hours of electricity per year, enough to power some 4,500 homes.

▶▶ *Nova Scotia*
People/Places/Things

Benjamin Franklin and Canadian mail

Do you know the important Canadian connection to Benjamin Franklin? In 1753, he was named joint deputy postmaster-general for the British colonies and opened the first post office in Canada in Halifax.

"Unofficial" flag

While Nova Scotia's flag had been used for 155 years, it wasn't recognized as the official flag of the province until 2013, when an 11-year-old girl realized that, while researching the flag for a school project, the flag hadn't actually been officially recognized by the provincial government. Once the error was brought to light, the flag was officially recognized under the Provincial Flag Act.

Island of horses

Sable Island, off the coast of Nova Scotia, is inhabited mainly by wild horses. While there are a handful of other small animals on the island, the only humans allowed to stay there are Parks Canada staff, researchers and the people who operate the weather station on the island.

First cross-Canada car trip

Are we there yet? The first cross-Canada car trip took 49 days. Writer Tom Wilby and driver/mechanic Jack Haney left Halifax on August 27, 1912, in an REO the Fifth (the fifth car designed by Ransom E. Olds), and arrived in Vancouver on October 14. During the journey, the duo travelled 298 km on their best day and just 19 km on their worst.

Largest historical reconstruction

The Fortress of Louisbourg, a national historic site located on Nova Scotia's Cape Breton Island, is the largest historical reconstruction in North America. First built in 1713, the settlement was besieged twice before being destroyed by the British in the 1760s. In 1961, the federal government committed $25 million to restore about one-quarter of the original village, which includes buildings, yards, gardens and streets, as well as part of the fortifications.

24

Yukon
Community

"Yukon" originated from the Gwich'in native word *Yuk-un-ah*, meaning "Great River."

Lone city

Whitehorse is Yukon's only city. Of the entire population of Yukon (35,874), 70 percent live in its capital, Whitehorse.

Gold route
The Yukon River was the main transportation hub used during the Klondike Gold Rush. By 1900, there were 23 active sternwheelers ferrying gold seekers downriver to Klondike and Dawson City.

First people in North America
The earliest known signs of humans in North America have been found in Yukon's Bluefish Caves. Remains found at the site were believed to have been from approximately 14,000 years ago, but in 2017, researchers at the University of Montreal used modern radiocarbon dating and have revised the settlement date to approximately 24,000 years ago, making it the oldest known archaeological site in North America. The tools found at the site are made with a stone technology reminiscent of the Dyuktai culture of Siberia.

Oldest continuously inhabited land
Yukon, along with Alaska, is the oldest continuously inhabited land in North America.

Westernmost community
The nation's most westerly community is Yukon's Beaver Creek. Located on the Alaska Highway at the 141st meridian, the community is home to the White River First Nations and considered to be Canada's gateway to Alaska.

▶▶ *Yukon*
Business/Industry

Discoverers of gold

The first discovery of gold in the Klondike region of Yukon was by Skookum Jim Mason, Dawson Charlie, and prospector George Carmack. In 1896, Jim and Charlie, both from the Tagish First Nation group, and Carmack happened upon a gold nugget the size of a dime in Rabbit Creek. The group's find was the catalyst for the massive influx of gold prospectors who rushed to stake a claim in a region that would soon become known as having the richest yield of gold in Yukon's history.

THE GOLDFIELDS

KLONDIKE

Free land

"Buy land, they're not making it anymore." — Mark Twain

Well, in Canada, there are places where you don't have to buy land because the government is giving it away. That's right; to encourage more farming in Canada's north, the Yukon government has a program in which Canadians interested in farming can get 65 ha of land with no money down.

Biggest gold rush

The biggest gold rush in Canadian history was the Klondike Gold Rush from 1897 to 1899. During that time, 40,000 fortune seekers made their way to gold fields near Dawson, Yukon. By the end of the rush, prospectors spent an estimated $50 million reaching the Klondike, an amount essentially equal to the value of the gold extracted during those years.

Big cleanup

Situated in south-central Yukon, just outside the town of Faro, sits what used to be the largest open-pit lead and zinc mine in the world — Faro Mine. The mine operated for 29 years, until it closed in 1998. The site is one of the most complex abandoned mine cleanups in Canada. The former mine is 25 km², an area roughly the size of Victoria, British Columbia.

▶▶ *Yukon*
People/Places/Things

Midnight Sun
In some parts of Yukon, you can sink into a chair and read a book outside into the wee hours of the night without the use of a flashlight. That's because in those areas Yukon is north of the Arctic Circle, and from June to September, the sun rises and stays high in the sky for weeks. Of course, it also means that in the winter months Yukon nights in those places can be never ending.

Panning for gold
Today anyone can still pan for gold in Yukon, as long as the land is designated as "vacant" and does not already have a staked claim by a prospector or miner. So, if you've got gold fever, head to Yukon — and don't forget your pan and shovel.

Westernmost point

Canada's westernmost point is Boundary Peak in Yukon, along the Yukon–Alaska border.

Toughest dog sled race

The Yukon Quest 1,000 mile international sled dog race, is the self-proclaimed "toughest sled dog race in the world." The 1,600 km competition runs each February between Whitehorse, Yukon, and Fairbanks, Alaska, along the historical Klondike Gold Rush route. Besides the great distance, racers face temperatures plunging to –40°C, winds up to 160 km per hour and steep mountain summits.

25

Northwest Territories
Community

The Northwest Territories became a part of Canada on July 15, 1870 (as the North-West Territories). The territories have changed much since then. At some point, it included all of Alberta, Saskatchewan and Yukon, as well as parts of Manitoba, Ontario and Quebec. Today it spans from the Mackenzie River to the Beaufort Sea. In Inuktitut, the Northwest Territories is called Nunatsiaq, meaning "beautiful land."

Ice superhighways

A road trip to remember. For most of the year, the lush and rolling landscape of the Northwest Territories is impassable due to its expansive lakes, rivers and looming boreal forests. But from December to April, the lakes and rivers freeze over to create five ice roads that link various communities on the outer edges of the Northwest Territories to the capital — the Yellowknife–Dettah Ice Road, Tlicho Winter Road, Inuvik–Aklavik Ice Road (pictured here), Tibbitt–Contwoyto Winter Road and Wrigley–Fort Good Hope Winter Road. Though none of these roads extend far enough to reach any of the communities inside Nunavut, the Tibbitt to Contwoyto Winter Road is built every January for heavy-haul truck drivers to use to bring supplies to mines north of Yellowknife via the frozen Contwoyto lake on the Nunavut border.

Road to the Arctic Ocean

In 2017, the Inuvik–Tuktoyaktuk Northwest Highway opened. It begins where the Dempster Highway ends in Inuvik, Northwest Territories, and extends for 138 km to Tuktoyaktuk, Northwest Territories, a small community on the coast of the Arctic Ocean, making the highway Canada's only road to the Arctic Ocean.

Arctic Circle highway

The 740 km Dempster Highway, opened on August 18, 1979, is the only Canadian road to the Arctic Circle. The road begins in Dawson, Yukon, and ends at Inuvik, Northwest Territories. The road has served as a supply route linking Yukon and the Northwest Territories to southern Canada.

Most official languages

A multilingual territory. The Northwest Territories has 11 official languages: Chipewyan, Cree, French, English, North and South Slavey, Gwich'in, Inuinnaqtun, Inuktitut, Inuvialuktun and Tlicho. It is the only territory or province in Canada to have so many different official languages.

Largest dark-sky preserve

Wood Buffalo National Park is the world's largest dark-sky preserve. The park was officially granted the dark-sky preserve designation in August 2013 by the Royal Astronomical Society of Canada for its work to preserve dark skies for the benefit of visitors and ecology.

Famed North-West Mounted Police

Before Canada had the RCMP, the North-West Mounted Police guarded the country's borders during the Klondike Gold Rush. Established in 1873, the outfit was started as a police force to protect and keep order in the North-West Territories.

Best place to view aurora borealis

For 200 nights each year, aurora borealis (also known as the northern lights) is visible to the naked eye from the Northwest Territories. Located right beneath the Earth's "auroral oval," a huge ring of aurora light activity above the Earth's geomagnetic north pole, the Northwest Territories is one of the best places in the world to view this spectacular light show. As such, the northern lights have become the area's biggest tourist attraction.

North America's largest diamond

In 2018 the Diavik mine unveiled a monster-sized yellow diamond, coming in at 552 carats. The record-setting find far outweighs the previous record holder, the Diavik Foxfire (found at the same mine), which was a comparatively puny 197 carats.

Diamond capital of North America

How's this for bling: The Northwest Territories, once best known for gold, has become the diamond capital of North America. The mines in the territory account for 87 percent of all diamonds mined in Canada, making the nation the world's third-largest producer of diamonds.

Largest diamond mine

Canada's largest diamond mine, Diavik, is located 300 km north of Yellowknife, Northwest Territories. Run as part of the Rio Tinto group of companies, the reserves are located in four kimberlite pipes. Since production began in 2003, more than 100 million carats of rough diamonds have been extracted.

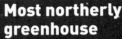

Most northerly greenhouse

Housed in an old hockey arena is the Inuvik Community Greenhouse, started in 1998 to provide fresh produce to Inuvik residents. Situated 200 km above the Arctic Circle, it is considered the world's most northerly commercial greenhouse. With only six to 10 weeks of summer annually, the greenhouse allows residents of Inuvik to grow their own vegetables, despite the never-ending night-time skies and extreme temperatures.

▶▶ *Northwest Territories*
People/Places/Things

Largest national park

It seems fitting that Canada's largest national park (and the second largest in the world) is named after North America's largest terrestrial animal. Wood Buffalo National Park, pictured here, straddles the Alberta–Northwest Territories border and spans 44,807 km². It was established in 1992 to protect the last remaining herds of the continent's wood bison.

Largest lake inside Canada

The Northwest Territories' Great Bear Lake is the biggest lake that is completely in Canada, and it is the eighth-largest lake in the world. It has an area of 31,792 km² and is 1,470 m deep at its deepest spot.

Loneliest park

At 170 km north of the Arctic Circle, Tuktut Nogait National Park is the least visited national park in the country, with only a handful of people venturing out to the park annually. Often referred to as "Canada's loneliest park," between 2010 and 2018, just 55 people travelled to the park, and in 2018 there were no visitors to the park. The lucky few who do brave the trip are treated to a view of the rare Bluenose-West caribou, raptors and grizzlies, as well as majestic hills, rivers and waterfalls.

Birthplace of hockey

The small town of Deline, Northwest Territories, considers itself the birthplace of hockey. While there are many who dispute this claim, this town on the shores of Great Bear Lake has the "receipts" to back up its claim to fame. In the 1820s, Arctic explorer Sir John Franklin and his men were stationed in Deline (then called Fort Franklin). In 1825, Franklin wrote to Britain, and in his letter, he details that his men were playing games of "hockey on the ice." This is known as the first recorded use of the name "hockey" to describe the game. In his diaries, Franklin also mentioned that "skating" was one of the winter "amusements" that helped his men pass the time in this new region. Whether, in fact, Franklin and his men were playing "hockey" while skating, the true form of the game beloved by Canadians today, still remains a mystery.

26

Nunavut | **Community**

The territory of Nunavut is named after the Inuktitut term meaning "our land."

First Arctic national park

The country's first national park north of the Arctic Circle is Nunavut's Auyuit-tuq National Park. Located on Baffin Island's Cumberland Peninsula, the 19,089 km² park was created as a national park reserve in 1976 and became a national park in 2001, as part of the Nunavut Land Claims Agreement.

Most northerly community

Grise Fiord, Nunavut, lays claim to the title of most northerly community in North America. Only about 150 people, mostly Inuit, live in the hamlet, which was established in 1953 when the federal government relocated Inuit families from northern Quebec and northern Baffin Island to this spot to strengthen Canadian claims to the High Arctic.

Youngest territory 1

Canada's largest territory is also the country's newest. Nunavut officially separated from the Northwest Territories on April 1, 1999, making it Canada's youngest territory.

Northernmost inhabited place

Alert, Nunavut, at latitude 82° 30' N, is the world's northernmost permanently inhabited place. Located on the northeastern coast of Ellesmere Island on the Lincoln Sea, Alert is the site of an Environment Canada weather station, an atmosphere observatory and a military station, which is occupied year-round by an unknown number of personnel. The settlement experiences 106 days of full darkness each year, and an average annual temperature of –18°C.

Youngest territory 2

Canada's newest territory also holds the country's lowest median age, 25.1 years, based on 2016 census data from Statistics Canada. Nearly one-third (32.5 percent) of the territory's residents are under the age of 15, truly making Nunavut Canada's youngest territory.

Business/Industry

Most northerly fly-in lodge

Adventurers can hike, bike, raft, paddleboard and much, much more at the Arctic Watch Wilderness Lodge, located on Somerset Island, Nunavut. Considered the world's most northerly fly-in lodge, it also has an Arctic library and interpretive centre with local artifacts and 42-million-year-old fossils.

First Arctic circus

Canada's first Arctic circus was born out of Igloolik, Nunavut. Co-founded in 1998, Artcirq is a collaboration of talented entertainers, young jugglers and acrobats who utilize Inuit traditions in their performances.

Northernmost mine

The planet's northernmost mine was the Polaris lead and zinc mine on Little Cornwallis Island in Nunavut. Before it closed in 2002, more than one million tonnes of ore were extracted annually. Its operators undertook 22 years of exploration before opening the mine in 1981. Along with the nearby Nanisivik lead and zinc mine, Polaris was one of the lowest-cost producers of zinc on the planet and made Nunavut the largest producer of zinc in Canada.

First bank branch in Canada's arctic

In 1957, the first bank branch to open in Canada's Arctic islands was a Royal Bank of Canada branch in Iqaluit, Nunavut (at the time, Frobisher Bay, Northwest Territories).

Nunavut's only green-energy-powered lodge

Weber Arctic operates the Arctic Watch Wilderness Lodge on Somerset Island, but it also runs its sister lodge, located on the shores of Ennadai Lake, Nunavut, where it is the territory's only completely green-powered lodge.

Bowhead whaling

On Kekerten Island lies Kekerten Territorial Park, an area first used as a whaling station by Scottish whaler William Penny in the mid-1800s. Located in the Cumberland Sound, the area was known as a hot spot for bowhead whales. The English and American whaling stations that appeared there over the decade utilized the knowledge and know-how of the local Inuit population, which decreased from more than 1,000 to less than 300 because of disease and work hazards. Today the park is a reminder of this bygone era, and includes the foundations of storehouses, rendering equipment for whale oil, a shipwreck and whale bones, like the bowhead jawbone seen here.

First Inuit-owned production company

Isuma Productions is Canada's first production company dedicated to exploring independent video art from an Inuit point of view. Founded in 1990, the company is 75 percent Inuit owned and has produced the world's only film ever written, directed and performed entirely in the Inuktitut language, *Atanarjuat: The Fast Runner*.

▶▶ *Nunavut*
People/Places/Things

Largest goose colony

By the sound of all the honking, you'd think it was one serious traffic jam. But no, it's just the world's largest goose colony, home to an estimated 1.7 million lesser snow geese. The federal Dewey Soper Migratory Bird Sanctuary on Nunavut's Baffin Island has an estimated one-third of all lesser snow geese on the planet, along with significant populations of other birds.

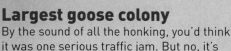

First Inuit Canadian Walk of Fame artist

In 2001, Kenojuak Ashevak made history when she became the first Inuit artist ever inducted into Canada's Walk of Fame. Often called "the grandmother of Inuit art," Ashevak became known for her vivid storytelling through her use of magic markers to create her artwork. Ashevak received many accolades: she was awarded the Order of Canada in 1967; in 1970 her print, *Enchanted Owl* (1960), was reproduced on a commemoration stamp celebrating the Northwest Territories, and in 1993 Canada Post selected her drawing *The Owl* for its 86-cent stamp. She died in 2013 at the age of 85.

Lone museum

The Nunatta Sunakkutaangit Museum is Nunavut's only provincially run museum. Opened in 1969, the museum is now housed in an old Hudson's Bay storage building, and its collection includes Inuit artifacts and artwork, as well as a collection of contemporary art pieces.

Northernmost point of Canada

Cape Columbia, Nunavut, is Canada's most northerly point of land.

Northernmost point of North America

It's certainly aptly named. Zenith Point, Nunavut, is the northernmost point of continental North America.

Largest protected lands

Nunavut has more protected land exceeding 1 million ha than any other region of Canada, including Qausuittuq National Park (1,108,000 ha), Ukkusiksalik National Park (1,765,786 ha), the Bylot Island Migratory Bird Sanctuary (1,937,361 ha), Auyuittuq National Park (1,793,200 ha), Quttinirpaaq National Park (3,543,300 ha) and Sirmilik National Park (2,197,800 ha).

Largest rodent

Know what Canada's largest rodent is? We're so proud of it we put it on our nickel, and it's celebrated as a symbol of Canadiana. Yes, the beaver — which can weigh as much as 35 kg and grow as long as 1.3 m (from nose to tail).

Largest beaver dam

DAM! The world's largest beaver dam (spotted on satellite images by the scientists who discovered it) is found in Wood Buffalo National Park.

Most polar bears

Canada has two-thirds of the Earth's population of polar bears, the world's largest terrestrial carnivore. Adult males average between 400 and 600 kg, with some exceeding 800 kg. Polar bears are also the largest species of bears.

Bird's deadliest enemies

Sorry cat lovers, but your cuddly kittens are actually brutal killers. According to a 2013 study by Environment Canada, predation by cats is the largest human-related cause of death for birds in Canada. Urban pet cats are estimated to be responsible for about one-sixth of all bird deaths in the country, while feral cats (just 25 percent of all cats) are responsible for 59 percent of bird deaths. Outdoor cats are estimated to be responsible for the deaths of between 105 and 348 million birds per year.

World's deadliest creature

Believe it or not, what many consider the world's deadliest creature lives right here in Canada. And they're found virtually everywhere. Fortunately for Canadians, the mosquito's bite here is largely just itchy, though it can transmit West Nile virus. Around the world, mosquito bites routinely kill two million people and transmit many diseases, including malaria, Zika virus and yellow fever.

Longest animal migration

The humpback whale makes the longest migration of any mammal on the planet. The species travels up to 8,500 km one way. The north Pacific population that travels through Canadian waters journeys from Alaska to the tropical seas off Hawaii.

Largest land animal

The largest land animal in North America is the wood bison, which can be found in Alberta, Manitoba and the Northwest Territories. Mature males can reach 3.8 m in length, stand 2 m high at the shoulder and weigh up to 900 kg. It's believed there were once more than 168,000 wood bison in Canada, but hunting and severe winters have decimated the population. Today the country is home to only about 10,000 of these animals.

►► *Animals*

Most common cow
The Holstein is the most common dairy cow breed in Canada, accounting for 94 percent of the country's cows.

Largest herd of wood bison
Wood Buffalo National Park, which straddles the border between Alberta and the Northwest Territories, is home to the world's largest herd of wood bison. Around 3,000 of North America's largest land mammal call the park home.

Most sharks
Ripley's Aquarium of Canada is home to the largest collection of sharks in North America. One of the facility's highlights is the Dangerous Lagoon, which features a 96 m tunnel walkway through a 2.84-million-litre tank, where you can see sand tiger sharks that measure 3 to 3.7 m.

Most snakes

If you've got ophidiophobia (a fear of snakes), DON'T stop here. Manitoba's Narcisse Wildlife Management Area has the largest concentration of snakes in the world. It's estimated that up to 70,000 snakes use hibernacula (hibernation sites) here, particularly the red-sided garter snake. The snakes emerge in massive wriggly masses on the first warm days of May. In fact, Mother's Day, of all days, is often a prime time to see the spectacle.

Largest animal on earth

The biggest animal on Earth calls Canada home (at least part of the time). Blue whales, which can grow up to 30 m long and weigh up to 200 tonnes, are found in Canadian waters along Canada's east coast. Not only are blue whales the largest creature on the planet, they're also the loudest. Their cry can reach 186 decibels — louder than a jet plane.

Freshwater harbour seals

In the Nunavik region of Quebec, about 250 km east of Hudson Bay, lies a very unique population of harbour seals — the planet's only population of the species that lives year-round in fresh water. Known as the Lac des Loups Marins harbour seals, experts believe the animals were separated from their original marine habitat 3,000 to 8,000 years ago. It's estimated that there are 100 of the seals, which are considered endangered.

Largest and oldest freshwater fish

The white sturgeon is the largest and longest-living freshwater fish in North America. In Canada, the species can be found in a number of rivers in British Columbia, including the Fraser, Kootenay, Nechako and Columbia. Specimens more than 6 m in length and estimated to be more than 100 years old have been recorded in the Fraser River.

Largest lake sturgeon

Another big fish story. The International Game Fish Association all-tackle world-record lake sturgeon was caught in Ontario's Georgian Bay on May 29, 1982. The behemoth weighed a whopping 76.2 kg.

Largest arctic grayling

Perhaps it should come as little surprise, given our expanse of Arctic, that the International Game Fishing Association all-tackle world record for Arctic grayling was caught in Canada. The record grayling was nabbed on August 16, 1967, in the Katseyedie River, Northwest Territories, and tipped the scales at 2.69 kg.

Largest lake whitefish

The International Game Fish Association all-tackle world-record lake whitefish was caught on May 21, 1984, in Meaford, Ontario. The fish weighed 6.52 kg.

*photos on these pages are samples of each species, and not the record-setting catches.

Largest rock bass

What a big red eye you have! One of the two fish tied for the International Game Fish Association all-tackle world-record rock bass — a species recognizable by its distinctive red eye — was caught in Ontario's York River on August 1, 1974. The rock bass weighed 1.36 kg.

Biggest salmon

With Canada's world-renowned salmon runs, is it any wonder the country holds a salmon-angling world record? The International Game Fish Association all-tackle world record for chum salmon, a 15.87 kg fish, was caught on July 11, 1995, in Edye Pass, British Columbia.

Largest aurora trout

It figures that the International Game Fish Association all-tackle world record for Aurora trout comes from Canada. The 2.22 kg fish was caught in Ontario's Carol Lake on October 8, 1996.

Unique brook trout

The Aurora trout, a unique strain of brook trout, is found only in Ontario and Quebec. The original strain of the fish was extirpated from its original native lakes in Ontario's Temagami region. Captive breeding led to the reintroduction of the species to a select group of lakes in the 1990s.

Largest brook trout

If you're an angler in Canada, you're undoubtedly familiar with the legendary Cook brook trout. Caught in July 1915 by Dr. J.W. Cook in Ontario's Nipigon River, the 6.6 kg brookie has stood as the world record for the species for nearly a century. In fact, it's one of the longest-standing angling records on Earth.

Largest splake

Given that it's somewhat of a uniquely Canadian species, it's hardly surprising that the International Game Fish Association all-tackle world record for splake was caught here. The 9.39 kg fish was hauled from Ontario's Georgian Bay on May 17, 1987.

Labrador Retriever

The Labrador retriever, which originated on the island of Newfoundland, was first recognized as a breed by England's Kennel Club in 1903, though records describing the breed date from as early as the mid-18th century. Known as a "water dog," Labs are appreciated for their intelligence and outgoing nature.

Tahltan Bear Dog

The Tahltan bear dog was the last of the five Canadian dog species recognized by the Canadian Kennel Club. The breed was used by the Tahltan Indians of northeastern British Columbia to hunt bear and lynx. Only nine were ever registered with the CKC after the breed was recognized in 1940, and today it is considered by authorities to be extinct.

Nova Scotia Duck Tolling Retriever

The Nova Scotia duck tolling retriever, the official dog of Nova Scotia, was the first Canadian dog breed to be named a provincial symbol. Developed in the early 19th century, the species was bred to lure (or toll) and retrieve waterfowl.

Newfoundland Dog

The Newfoundland dog is another made-in-Canada dog species. Little is known of the breed's exact origins, though the species was first named in the late 17th century. Nearly as at home in the water — if not more so — than on the land, the Newfoundland was originally used as a ship dog (to carry lines to shore or for water rescues).

Canadian Eskimo Dog

This is one old dog. The Canadian Eskimo Dog is considered the oldest indigenous dog species still in existence. The breed, often used to pull sleds, is believed to have originated around 1100 to 1200 AD in what is now the Canadian Arctic. The breed, also known as the Canadian Inuit Dog, is the official animal of Nunavut.

First migratory waterfowl refuge system

Jack Miner, known as "the Father of Conservation," is considered the founder of the migratory waterfowl refuge system. He founded the first such reserve, the Jack Miner Migratory Bird Sanctuary, in 1904 in Kingsville, Ontario.

First banded birds

Five years after Jack Miner established the world's first migratory bird reserve, he created the concept of banding birds to trace the migratory periods and routes of waterfowl. Ever since, the practice has been instrumental in the protection of migratory birds in North America and the world.

BRANT GEESE

Longest bird migration

Too bad there are no frequent flyer miles for birds. If there were, the Arctic tern would earn lots of free flights. After all, the small seabird, which summers in Canada's north, has the longest migration of any bird in the world. It travels some 40,000 km from its Arctic breeding grounds to its winter home near Antarctica and back again.

Largest number of bald eagles

You don't need to be eagle-eyed to spy the famous birds that flock to British Columbia's Brackendale Eagle Provincial Park from November to February each year. That's because the park is home to the continent's largest concentration of bald eagles. Indeed, in 1994, there was a world-record count of 3,769 eagles. The count fluctuates greatly, and that is because it is largely dependent on food availability and water levels during the salmon run. In 2016 there was an all-time low of 411 bald eagles. In 2019 sightings jumped to 1,157.

Whooping cranes

Wood Buffalo National Park is home to the original nesting site of this endangered species. There are approximately 220 birds nesting in Canada at Wood Buffalo. They migrate to the Gulf Coast in the United States in the winter. An additional flock of American whooping cranes nests in Idaho and migrates to New Mexico, while a non-migrating flock calls Florida home.

Largest bird sanctuary

If birds have a heaven on Earth, it must be the Queen Maud Gulf Migratory Bird Sanctuary on the Arctic Ocean coast in Nunavut. It's the country's largest migratory bird sanctuary and Canada's largest federally protected area, measuring approximately 61,765 km². There are about 60 goose colonies in the area (including Brant geese, pictured here). One contains 90 percent of the world population of Ross' geese and another has more than 30 percent of the Western Canadian Arctic population of lesser snow geese.

Canada's beetle

Found only in eastern North America, the checkered beetle is 8 to 11 mm long and has red, orange or red checkered spots. This pollinator will sometimes feed on wood-boring insects and live where there are good supplies of nectar and pollen.

Glow in the dark

Did you know that it's believed that 29 different species of firefly and lightning bugs call Canada home? And guess what? These bugs aren't flies at all — they're beetles. Now that's illuminating!

The good-luck bug

In Canada some believe a ladybug hibernating in your shed or garage is good luck! In England, farmers believed a ladybug sighting was the sign of a good harvest. In truth, there are 450 native species of ladybug in North America. And while they may not be lucky, they are certainly pretty — you can even tell what kind of ladybug you've seen by counting the spots!

Canada's butterfly

First named in 1906, the Canadian Tiger Swallowtail is very similar to the Eastern Tiger Swallowtail. The Canadian butterfly is slightly smaller than its eastern counterpart, though it is still a fairly large butterfly, with a wingspan of 53 to 90 mm. The Canadian Tiger Swallowtail is found in every province and territory and can be found as far north as the Arctic Circle!

Longest butterfly migration

It weighs about as much as a paper clip, but the monarch butterfly doesn't let its small size get in the way of travelling great distances. The monarch butterfly makes the longest migration of all insect species. Experts believe that monarchs travel at least 4,600 km, but it's possible that they fly twice as far as that. Individuals migrate from southern Canada to wintering areas in Mexico each fall.

Dinosaurs & Fossils

Newly discovered tyrannosaur

Not far from Dinosaur Provincial Park an amateur fossil hunter, John De Groot, found a well-preserved jaw bone of what is now known as *Thanatotheristes degrootorum*, a 79.5-million-year-old tyrannosaur, and the first of its kind found in the world. The newly identified species, named after *Thanatos* (the Greek god of death) and *theristes* (one who reaps or harvests), was roughly 9 m long and weighed about 2,000 kg. It is the oldest of the tyrannosaur species, and one of five ever discovered in Canada; the others are: *Daspletosaurus*, *Gorgosaurus*, *Albertosaurus* and *Tyrannosaurus*.

Most dinosaur fossils

Where will you find the richest area of dinosaur fossils in the world? Why, Alberta's Dinosaur Provincial Park, naturally. Since the 1880s, more than 150 complete dinosaur skeletons have been unearthed from a 27 km area near the Red Deer River. More than 50 dinosaur species have been found here, as well as the fossils of 450 other organisms.

Oldest fossils

Canada is home to three of the world's known examples of the oldest fossils on the planet — signs of the earliest life on Earth. Known as stromatolites, these fossils, which date back 3 to 3.5 billion years ago, are very rare. Examples have been found near Red Lake and Steep Rock Lake, Ontario, and near Yellowknife, Northwest Territories.

Oldest shark fossil

The world's oldest intact shark fossil was discovered in 1997 near Atholville, New Brunswick. The 23 cm long fossil (from snout to upper trunk), which includes the fish's braincase, scales, calcified cartilage, large fin spines and teeth, is estimated to be more than 400 million years old, which is five million years older than the second-oldest known specimen.

Largest fossil

Like dinosaurs? Like bugs? This is for you! The world's largest known complete fossil of a trilobite, a prehistoric multilegged sea creature, was found along Hudson Bay in Manitoba. The specimen is from the largest-known species of trilobites, *Isotelus rex*, and it resembles a huge bug and is more than 70 cm long.

▶▶ Dinosaurs & Fossils

Most petroglyphs and pictographs

Alberta's Writing-on-Stone Provincial Park, located in the southeast corner of the province, is home to the largest concentration of First Nation petroglyphs (rock carvings) and pictographs (rock paintings) on the Great Plains of North America.

Biggest marine dinosaur

What a big mosasaur you have! The prehistoric marine dinosaur, from the late Cretaceous period 80 million years ago, on display at the Canadian Fossil Discovery Centre in Morden, Manitoba, is the largest of its kind on display in the world. Nicknamed Bruce (though it's actually a female), the beast measures more than 13 m in length.

Most dinosaurs

Looking for dinosaur bones? The Royal Tyrrell Museum of Paleontology, near Drumheller, Alberta, has one of the largest displays of dinosaurs on Earth. It's Canada's only museum dedicated to paleontology. The museum, which opened September 25, 1985, is named after Joseph Burr Tyrrell, who discovered the *Albertosaurus* (pictured here) in 1884, not far from the museum's site near Kneehill Creek.

Largest *T.rex*

Found outside Eastend, Saskatchewan, in 1991, Scotty is the biggest *Tyrannosaurus rex* ever unearthed. Discovered by a team from the Royal Saskatchewan Museum, Scotty is 13 m long and weighed an estimated 8,800 kg.

Oldest reptiles

The fossils of the reptiles whose descendants would become dinosaurs and mammals can be found at the Joggins Fossil Cliffs in Nova Scotia. These 315-million-year-old fossils are the world's oldest-known reptiles. They come from a time when giant seed fern trees, insects, primitive lobe-finned fish and amphibians roamed the Earth. The fossils are visible simply from a walk on Joggins beach.

29 ▶ *Geography*

Hydrographic apex

The hydrographic apex of North America — the only spot on the continent where water flows to three different oceans from one point — is the Columbia Icefield in Alberta's Jasper National Park.

Largest crater

The largest known impact crater in Canada (and the second largest on Earth) is found near Sudbury, Ontario. Known as the Sudbury Basin, the crater is 250 km in diameter. It is believed that the impact of a 10 km meteorite created the Sudbury Basin in just seconds about 1.85 million years ago.

Mars on Earth

About the closest environment to Mars that exists on the Earth is that of the Haughton Crater in Nunavut. It is a polar desert that undergoes little erosion because of the relative lack of water or vegetation. NASA has used this area to prepare for Mars expeditions and test its Mars rovers, like the K10 Rover "Red."

Largest non-polar icefield

Yukon's Seward Glacier and Alaska's Bagley Icefield together form the largest non-polar icefield in the world. The area is home to some of the world's longest and most spectacular glaciers. The icefields are a United Nations Educational, Scientific and Cultural Organization (UNESCO) world heritage site that combines Kluane National Park and Reserve in Yukon and Tatshenshini–Alsek Provincial Park in British Columbia with Wrangell–St. Elias National Park and Glacier Bay National Park in Alaska.

Largest dune formation

Ontario's Sandbanks Provincial Park, on the shores of Lake Ontario near Picton, is home to the largest baymouth-barrier dune formation in the world. Some sections of the dune are 60 m high. The park's location and unique habitat make it a hot spot for migrating birds in the spring and fall.

Largest dune field

Think of long, sandy beaches and you probably don't think of Canada. You also probably don't think of Canada's north. But the Athabasca Sand Dunes, a series of dune fields running about 100 km along the south shore of Lake Athabasca in northwest Saskatchewan, is the largest active sand dune surface in Canada and one of the most northern dune fields on Earth.

►► Geography

Largest wetland

The Hudson Bay Lowland is the largest wetland area in North America and the third largest on Earth. Eighty-three percent of the ecozone lies in Ontario, with smaller portions in neighbouring Quebec and Manitoba. More than 85 percent of the region is mineral wetland or organic peat land. The area has very few trees.

Largest continuous wetland

The Columbia Wetlands, located on the Upper Columbia River in the East Kootenays area of British Columbia, are considered the largest continuous wetlands in North America. The wetlands cover some 15,000 ha over a 150 km stretch, from Canal Flats and Invermere to Golden.

Largest freshwater ecosystem

Looking for fresh water? Look no further than the Great Lakes. Lake Ontario, Lake Erie, Lake Huron, Lake Michigan and Lake Superior form the world's largest freshwater ecosystem. It's estimated that a drop of water takes 400 years to travel from the system's headwaters in Lake Superior to the point where Lake Ontario meets the St. Lawrence River. The Great Lakes basin contains about 20 percent of the world's surface fresh water.

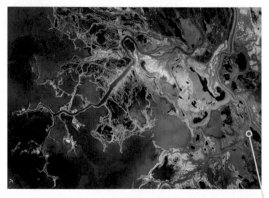

Largest freshwater delta (world)

The globe's largest inland freshwater delta is found in Wood Buffalo National Park.

Largest inland freshwater delta

While such things are debatable because of the range of criteria on which they're based, nonetheless the Global Institute for Water Security considers the Saskatchewan River Delta — a series of lakes, rivers and wetlands along the Saskatchewan–Manitoba border — to be the largest inland freshwater delta in North America and one of the largest in the world. This river delta is also known as one of the most biologically diverse regions in the country.

Largest collective body of fresh water

The Great Lakes cover more than 240,000 km². The freshwater system is so large that its natural features can be seen from the moon.

One-third of Earth's fresh water

The province where the Great Lakes are found, Ontario (which is also home to more than 250,000 other lakes), contains about one-third of the Earth's fresh water.

Longest river system

It could be the nation's longest winding trail. The Mackenzie River system is Canada's longest waterway, from its origins in the Columbia Icefields in Alberta's Jasper National Park and the deep snowfields of the upper Peace River in northeastern British Columbia to its mouth on the Beaufort Sea of the Arctic Ocean on Nunavut's coast. Including all the rivers and lakes of the system's 1.8 million km² drainage basin, it stretches 4,241 km in total, ranking as the world's 13th-longest river system.

Canada's longest rivers

4,241 km	1. Mackenzie, Northwest Territories
3,060 km	**2. St. Lawrence, Quebec/Ontario**
2,575 km	3. Nelson, Manitoba
1,939 km	4. Saskatchewan, Saskatchewan
1,923 km	5. Peace, British Columbia/Alberta
1,610 km	6. Churchill, Alberta/Saskatchewan/Manitoba
1,538 km	7. Athabasca, Alberta
1,370 km	8. Fraser, British Columbia
1,270 km	9. Ottawa, Quebec/Ontario
1,150 km	10. Yukon (Canadian portion only), British Columbia/Yukon

▶▶ *Geography*

Canada's 10 largest lakes

1. Lake Superior, ON
2. Lake Huron, ON
3. Great Bear Lake, NWT
4. Great Slave Lake, NWT
5. Lake Erie, MB
6. Lake Winnipeg, MB
7. Lake Ontario, ON
8. Lake Athabasca, SK
9. Reindeer Lake, SK/MB
10. Smallwood Reservoir, NL

Second-largest glacier-fed lake

Located in Alberta's Jasper National Park, Maligne Lake is the second-largest glacier-fed lake in the world. The lake is 22 km long and 97 m deep.

Salty lake

Water so buoyant it's impossible to sink? Head to the Dead Sea, right? Or go to central Saskatchewan's Little Manitou Lake. Fed by underground springs, the 13.3 km² lake has mineral salt concentrations of 180,000 mg per litre, making the water extremely buoyant.

Deepest lake

At 614 m deep, Great Slave Lake in the Northwest Territories is North America's deepest lake. The 8,568 km² lake is also the fourth-largest lake in Canada.

Highest point of departure

It seems hard to believe, but there's a lake in central Ontario that's the highest fresh-water lake in the Americas from which a skipper can circumnavigate the world by ocean-going vessel. At 265.5 m above sea level, Ontario's Balsam Lake is considered the "summit" of the Trent-Severn Waterway, a canal system that crosses Ontario's cottage country from Lake Ontario's Bay of Quinte to Lake Huron's Georgian Bay.

Most Canadian Great lake

Canada shares four of the Great Lakes with the United States (Lake Michigan is wholly in the United States). But do you know which Great lake has the largest portion in Canada? Lake Huron, with a total of 36,000 of its 59,600 km² located north of the border.

More lakes

There are millions of lakes in Canada, so it's hardly surpris-ing that our nation has more lake area than any other country. They're often big, too, with 563 lakes larger than 100 km².

▶▶ Geography

Largest mountain park

Looking for a park full of mountains? Look no further than Alberta's Jasper National Park, the largest mountain national park in the country. The 11,228 km² park boasts stunning mountain vistas, a plethora of wildlife and more than 1,200 km of hiking trails.

Largest erratic

A big rock, indeed. Known as "the Big Rock," the Okotoks Erratic (a rock moved from its original location by a glacier) is the largest-known glacial erratic in the world. Weighing an estimated 16,500 tonnes and measuring about 9 m high, 41 m long and 18 m wide, the Big Rock is located southwest of Okotoks, Alberta. It's believed the erratic was originally part of a mountain in what is now Jasper National Park, some 450 km away.

Perfect peak

It's Canada's perfect peak. British Columbia's Mount Assiniboine (3,618 m) is considered comparable to the Matterhorn in Switzerland due to its nearly symmetrical pyramid shape.

The most pingos

Our pingos are bigger than yours. The Northwest Territories' Mackenzie Delta region is home to the world's greatest concentration of pingos (some 1,350) and one of the largest in the world. A pingo is an ice-cored hill, usually conically shaped, that grows only in permafrost. They're formed when water freezing under the surface is forced up by pressure, and they range from a few metres to several tens of metres high.

Highest pingo

The Ibyuk Pingo, near Tuktoyaktuk, Northwest Territories, is the highest pingo (a unique ice-core formation) in Canada and the second largest in the world. It pokes up 49 m above the surrounding terrain.

Highest mountains

Nine of Canada's 10 highest mountains are in Yukon, including the highest — Mount Logan.

	Name	Height (m)	Location
1.	**Mount Logan, Yukon**	**5,959**	**60.567 / −140.403**
2.	Mount Saint Elias, Yukon	5,489	60.293 / −140.929
3.	Mount Lucania, Yukon	5,226	61.022 / −140.463
4.	King Peak, Yukon	5,173	60.583 / −140.654
5.	Mount Steele, Yukon	5,073	61.093 / −140.3
6.	Mount Wood, Yukon	4,842	61.233 / −140.512
7.	Mount Vancouver, Yukon	4,812	60.359 / −139.698
8.	Moung Slaggard, Yukon	4,742	61.173 / −140.584
9.	Mount Fairweather, British Columbia	4.663	58.910 / −137.541
10.	Mount Hubbard, Yukon	4,557	60.319 / −139.071

▶▶ *Geography*

Niagara Falls

Most impressive waterfalls

It's been said Ontario's famous Niagara Falls are the world's largest by volume. However, that is simply not true. They may, however, be the globe's most impressive, with more than 168,000 m³ of water going over the edge every minute. The falls have moved back 11 km in 12,500 years due to erosion and may be the world's fastest-moving waterfalls.

Highest waterfalls

James Bruce Falls, BC, 840 m
Gold Creek Falls, BC, 610 m
Madden Falls, BC, 579 m
Rugged Glacier Falls, BC, 560 m
Daniels River Falls, BC, 540 m
Swiftcurrent Falls, BC, 537 m
Marion Falls, BC, 527 m
Schwarzenbach Falls, NU, 520 m
Della Falls, BC, 440 m

Largest island

With millions of lakes across the country and the longest coastline in the world, Canada is also home to thousands, if not millions, of islands. Most Canadians, however, are unlikely to ever see the nation's largest island, Nunavut's Baffin Island, which lies in the Arctic Ocean north of Labrador. At 507,451 km², Baffin is also the fifth-largest island in the world. Nunavut's capital, Iqaluit, is located on the island's southern coast on Frobisher Bay.

Largest uninhabited island

Nunavut's Devon Island claims to be the largest island on Earth uninhabited by people. Located just north of Baffin Island, about one-third of Devon's 55,247 km² is covered by ice, while the rest of the island is largely barren.

Island-lake-island-lake-island

Okay, follow closely: Canada is home to the world's largest island, in a lake, on an island, in a lake, on an island. About 120 km inland from the southern coast of Nunavut's portion of Victoria Island, the 1 ha, nameless island is found on a small lake that's on an island surrounded by a smaller lake.

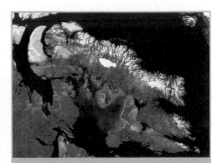

Canada's 10 largest islands

1. Baffin Island, Nunavut, 507,451 km²
2. Victoria Island, Nunavut/Northwest Territories, 217,291 km²
3. Ellesmere Island, Nunavut, 196,236 km²
4. Newfoundland, 111,390 km²
5. Banks Island, Northwest Territories, 70,028 km²
6. Devon Island, Nunavut, 55,247 km²
7. Axel Heiberg Island, Nunavut, 43,178 km²
8. Melville Island, Northwest Territories/Nunavut, 42,149 km²
9. Southampton Island, Nunavut, 41,214 km²
10. Prince of Wales Island, Nunavut, 33,339 km²

Largest lake on an island

Baffin Island is not only Canada's largest island, but it's also home to the world's largest lake on an island. Measuring some 5,542 km², Nettilling Lake is the largest lake in Nunavut and the 11th largest in Canada. It is located toward the island's south end, about 110 km southwest of Auyuittuq National Park. Covered by ice for most of the year, the lake is known to host only three fish species: Arctic char and two species of stickleback.

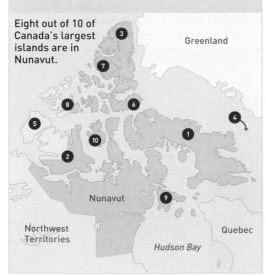

Eight out of 10 of Canada's largest islands are in Nunavut.

Greenland

Nunavut

Northwest Territories

Quebec

Hudson Bay

Lake in a lake

A lake in a lake? You bet. Ontario's Manitoulin Island is home to the world's largest lake on a freshwater island (and the world's largest lake in a lake, too). Lake Manitou has a surface area of approximately 104 km². There are also a number of small islands on Manitou, making them islands on a lake on an island in a lake!

▶▶ *Geography*

First marine park

Fathom Five National Marine Park was Canada's first national marine park. Established in 1987, the park covers a 130 km² area of water and 20 islands located off the end of Ontario's Bruce Peninsula, which separates Lake Huron from Georgian Bay. The park's waters are home to unique geology, plants and wildlife as well as 22 shipwrecks.

Largest karst

This is one impressive drain. The Maligne Valley karst is the largest-known underground drainage system in the country. Located in Alberta's Jasper National Park, the drainage includes Medicine Lake and Maligne Canyon.

Largest hot springs

The hot springs in the village of Radium Hot Springs, British Columbia, are the largest in the country. The pool's water, maintained at a temperature of 39°C, is odourless and clear.

Largest provincial park

More than four times the size of Prince Edward Island, Quebec's Parc national Tursujuq is the largest provincial park in the country. The 26,107 km² park, located on the eastern shore of Hudson Bay, was created on December 14, 2012.

Highest Arctic land area

Canada's Arctic Archipelago is the largest high-Arctic land area in the world, apart from Greenland (which is almost entirely covered in ice and geologically part of the archipelago). The chain is made up of 94 islands larger than 130 km² and 36,469 smaller islands. It has six of the world's 30 largest islands.

"Great" Canadian places

These are literally "Great" Canadian places:

- Great Barachois Lake, NS
- Great Barasway Lookout, NL
- Great Barasway Pond, NL
- Great Barren Lake, NS
- Great Bear Creek, BC
- Great Bear Lake, NT
- Great Bear River, NT
- Great Beaver Lake, BC
- Great Black Island, NL
- Great Brook, NL
- Great Burnt Island, NL
- Great Buse Bay, NL
- Great Calf Island, NS
- Great Chain Island, BC
- Great Coat Island, NL
- Great Colinet Island, NL
- Great Cormorandier Island, NL
- Great Denier Island, NL
- Great Duck Island, NB
- Great Duck Island, ON
- Great Eastern Pond, NL
- Great Falls, NS
- Great Falls, MB
- Great French Beach, NL
- Great Gulch River, NL
- Great Gull Lake, NL
- Great Gull River, NL
- Great Hill, NS
- Great Island, NL
- Great Island, NS
- Great Island, MB
- Great Jervis Island, NL
- Great La Cloche Island, ON
- Great Lake, ON
- Great Manitou Island, ON
- Great Mountain, NL
- Great Mountain Lake, ON
- Great Northern Mountain, NL
- Great Pike Lake, ON
- Great Pine Lake, NS
- Great Pond, NB
- Great Pond, NL
- Great Portage Lake, ON
- Great Pubnico Lake, NS
- Great Rattling Brook, NL
- Great Ridge, NS
- Great Rock Peak, BC
- Great Sacred Island, NL
- Great Sand Hills, SK
- Great Seal Island, NL
- Great Slave Lake, NT
- Great Snow Mountain, BC
- Great Thrum, NS
- Great Tinker Island, NL
- Great Verdon Island, NL
- Great Village River, NS
- Great West Ridge, AB

Snowiest May

At an average of 54 days with at least 2 mm of snow, Calgary, Alberta, just barely doesn't make the list as one of the country's biggest cities with most days of fresh snow. That said, it receives more snow in May, September and October than any other Canadian city. On average, Calgary has two to three days of snow in May, one or two in September and four (!) in October.

Biggest snowfall in one year

The heaviest annual snowfall the country has witnessed was in the Revelstoke–Mount Copeland area of British Columbia. The region spent the winter of 1971–72 digging out from a total of 2,446.5 cm, or nearly 24.5 m of snow.

Major cities outside of BC with the least snow

Saskatoon tops this list of least snowiest major cities in the country, outside of British Columbia.

City	inches	cm
Saskatoon, SK	35.9	91.3
Brantford, ON	38.7	98.4
Regina, SK	39.4	100.2
Oshawa, ON	41.6	105.8
Winnipeg, MB	44.8	113.7
Toronto, ON	47.8	121.5

Snowiest communities

Canada's snowiest communities outside of British Columbia based on average annual snowfall.

Days	Place	inches	cm
89	Woody Point, NL	251.1	638.0
117	Forêt Montmorency, QC	244.1	619.9
125	Cape Dyer, NU	218.2	554.2
85	Murdochville, QC	215.7	547.8
103	St. Anthony, NL	214.0	543.7
51	Main Brook, NL	202.8	515.0

Biggest blizzards

Canada's biggest blizzards, based on biggest single-day snowfalls on record:

Date	Place	inches	cm
February 11, 1999	Tahtsa Lake West, BC	57.1	145.0
December 4, 1985	Pleasant Camp, BC	50.0	127.0
March 20, 1885	Cap-de-la-Madeleine, QC	48.0	121.9
January 17, 1974	Lakelse Lake, BC	46.5	118.0
February 11, 1999	Terrace, BC	44.6	113.4
February 18, 1972	Kitimat, BC	44.2	112.3
January 16, 1976	Stewart, BC	41.6	105.7
February 5, 1988	Main Brook, NL	41.3	105.0
January 11, 1968	Kemano, BC	41.0	104.1
January 27, 2000	Unuk River, Eskay Creek Mine, BC	40.9	104.0
January 6, 1988	Nain, NL	40.7	103.4
February 17, 1943	Colinet, NL	40.0	101.6

Most months of snow

Snow, snow, go away. Ten of the nation's largest cities have at least 1 cm of snow on the ground for at least three months (or more than 120 days).

Average number of days a year when snow is 1 cm or more deep:

	City	Days
1.	Saguenay, QC	155
2.	Quebec City, QC	141
3.	Sudbury, ON	136
4.	Trois-Rivières, QC	134
5.	Sherbrooke, QC	133
6.	Edmonton, AB	133
7.	Winnipeg, MB	128
8.	Thunder Bay, ON	126
9.	Regina, SK	125
10.	Saskatoon, SK	124

Snowiest cities

When it comes to snow in Canada's largest cities, 10 of them receive an average of more than 2 m of the white stuff annually (based on urban centres with more than 100,000 population in 2011 and snow data averages between 1981 and 2010).

Annual average snowfall a year:

City	inches	cm
St. John's NL	131.9	335.0
Saguenay, QC	126.6	321.7
Quebec City, QC	119.4	303.4
Sherbrooke, QC	112.8	286.5
Moncton, NB	111.0	282.0
Sudbury, ON	103.7	263.4
Trois-Rivières, QC	102.0	259.0
Saint John, NB	94.3	239.6
Barrie, ON	87.8	223.0
Montreal, QC	82.5	209.5

Maritime community with the highest snowfall

A snow blower must be standard equipment for a homeowner in Woody Point, Newfoundland. Located on Bonne Bay on the province's west coast, Woody Point has received the highest recorded average snowfall of the Atlantic provinces. Over 89 days, 638 cm of snow falls each year.

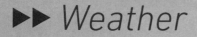

▶▶ Weather

Highest average snowfall

The highest average annual snowfall ever recorded at an Environment Canada weather station is 1,388 cm on Mount Fidelity, British Columbia. This mountain in Glacier National Park averages 141 days of snow a year.

Days	Place	inches	cm
141	Mount Fidelity, Glacier National Park, BC	546.4	1388.0
114	Unuk River, Eskay Creek Mine, BC	511.3	1298.6
104	Tahtsa Lake West, BC	384.1	975.7
78	Grouse Mountain, North Vancouver, BC	342.0	868.7
112	Rogers Pass, BC	340.4	864.7
78	Pleasant Camp, BC	285.0	723.8
90	Fraser Camp, BC	276.8	703.2
69	Hollyburn Ridge, West Vancouver, BC	257.7	654.6

Toronto's worst snowfall

There was that time Toronto called in the army (early January 1999), but the worst single-day snowfall in the country's largest city was actually December 11, 1944. The winter storm dropped 48 cm of snow on Toronto. In all, 57.2 cm of snow fell over two days, and 21 people died, including 13 from overexertion.

Toronto's snowiest January

Lest Toronto get too bad a rap for calling in the army, the series of snowstorms that struck the city from January 2 to 15, 1999, dropped almost a year's worth of snow over those two weeks. In total, it was the snowiest January in the city's history, with 118.4 cm of snow and the most snow on the ground at one time, at 65 cm.

Biggest single-day snowfall in a Canadian capital

St. John's, Newfoundland, grabbed this title on January 17, 2020, when the region was walloped by a severe winter storm that dumped 76.2 cm (30 inches) in one day, as recorded at St. John's International Airport. The storm caused an eight-day state of emergency in the city, and hundreds of troops from the Canadian Armed Forces were called in to help dig out the capital.

Cities with the least frequency of snow

City	Days
Victoria, BC	7
Vancouver, BC	9
Abbotsford, BC	12
Kelowna, BC	21
Brantford, ON	24
Halifax, NS	25
Oshawa, ON	27
Saskatoon, SK	28
Peterborough, ON	34
Hamilton, ON	36

Montreal's worst snowstorm

Montreal gets a lot of snow. The worst snowstorm to hit the city happened on March 4, 1971. In total, 43 cm of snow hit the city, and 110 km per hour winds created snow drifts as high as two storeys. The storm created power outages that lasted up to 10 days in some areas, and 17 people died as a result of the blizzard.

Longest-lasting snowfall

Outside of Canada's territories, here are the places with the highest number of average days each year with at least 1 cm of snow on the ground:

Location	Days
Alert, Nunavut	304
St. John's, NL	79
Sherbrooke, QC	76
Sudbury, ON	75
Quebec City, QC	70
Thunder Bay, ON	62
Kitchener-Waterloo, ON	62
London, ON	60
Montreal, QC	59
Regina, SK	56
Saguenay, QC	49

Biggest single-day snowfall

Get the shovel, er, shovels! The greatest single-day snowfall recorded in Canada was February 11, 1999, when Tahtsa, British Columbia, was blanketed with nearly a metre and a half of the white stuff (145 cm, to be exact). That broke a record of 118.1 cm of snow that fell on Lakelse Lake, British Columbia, on January 17, 1974. Neither is near the world record of 192 cm, set at Silver Lake, Colorado, on April 15, 1921.

►► *Weather*

Ice storm of the century

Some called it "the storm of the century." Whatever you consider it, the ice storm that hit Quebec and Ontario starting on January 5, 1998, was the costliest winter storm in Canadian history. According to the Insurance Bureau of Canada, the six days of freezing rain led to month-long power outages in some locations and $2 billion (in 2011 dollars) in insured losses.

Coldest big city

Saguenay, Quebec, holds the record for the coldest major Canadian city, based on mean daily temperature averaged over a year, at 2.4°C. Winterpeg, er, Winnipeg, is actually the fifth-coldest major city at 5.0°C, following Regina at 2.8°C, Saskatoon at 3.5°C and Edmonton at 3.8°C. Based on daily average temperature in just the months of December, January and February, the list changes:

City	Daily average °C
Winnipeg, MB	-15.3
Saskatoon, SK	-14.8
Saguenay, QC	-14.3
Regina, SK	-13.8
Sudbury, ON	-11.5
Quebec City, QC	-10.3
Edmonton, AB	-9.3
Sherbrooke, QC	-8.9

Lowest temperature

Brrr. The lowest temperature ever recorded in Canada and North America? The village of Snag, Yukon, registered -63°C on February 3, 1947.

Cold in 1947

Northwestern Canada experienced a particularly cool year in 1947. Check out these other Canadian low temperature records:

Location	°C	Date
Mayo, YT	-62.2	February 3, 1947
Watson Lake, YT	-58.9	January 31, 1947
Norman Wells, NWT	-54.4	February 4, 1947
Whitehorse, YT	-52.2	January 31, 1947
Fort Nelson, BC	-51.7	January 30, 1947
Dease Lake, BC	-51.2	January 31, 1947
Yellowknife, NWT	-51.2	January 31, 1947
Fort McMurray, AB	-50.6	February 1, 1947

Coldest days not in 1947

Location	°C	Date
Old Crow, YT	-59.4	January 5, 1975
Iroquois Falls, ON	-58.3	January 23, 1935
Shepherd Bay, NWT	-57.8	February 13, 1973
Inuvik, NWT	-56.7	February 4, 1968
Prince Albert, SK	-56.7	February 1, 1893
Dawson, YT	-55.8	February 11, 1979
Eureka, NU	-55.3	February 15, 1979

Winterpeg

Turns out Winnipeg leads when it comes to the average number of days when the temperature doesn't break 0°C, at 117. Perhaps it's not surprising that Saskatoon and Saguenay, Quebec, are second and third in the same category, with 112 and 110 days, respectively.

Coldest year

It seems fair to call it Canada's coldest year: in 1972, every weather-reporting station in the country reported annual temperatures below average, the only time on record this ever happened.

Coldest wind chill

Canadians know that frigid temperatures are one thing, but wind chill is another. The nation's record wind chill was set on January 28, 1989, at Kugaaruk, Nunavut (formerly Pelly Bay, Northwest Territories). The temperature was a nippy –51°C. The wind chill? A super-frosty –91°C!

Coldest cities

Canada's coldest city? A tie between Saskatoon and Regina, with –50°C recorded on February 1, 1893, and January 1, 1885, respectively.

Canada is pretty cool

Canada is just about the coolest country—literally. It vies with Russia for first place as the coldest nation in the world, with an average daily annual temperature of –5.6°C.

▶▶ *Weather*

Biggest one-hour mercury jump

There's a saying in Canada that if you don't like the weather, wait five minutes. Never could that have been truer than in Pincher Creek, Alberta, where Canada's most extreme temperature change was recorded. The mercury soared from –19°C to 22°C in just one hour.

Rainiest, foggiest, windiest

Cold, foggy and windy. Sounds like St. John's? Okay, it may be an unfair gener-alization, but of all Canadian cities, St. John's has the most days per year with freezing rain (38) and fog (121), and the most wind (an average annual wind speed of 24 km per hour).

Calmest city

Don't go fly a kite — at least not in Kelowna, British Columbia, because chances are slim you'll have enough wind for liftoff. Kelowna is Canada's least windy city, with 39 percent of wind observations per year indi-cating calm conditions.

Foggiest place in the world

The Grand Banks off Newfoundland is consid-ered the foggiest place in the world. The area experi-ences 40 percent fog cover in the winter and up to 84 percent in the summer.

Windiest place

Hold onto your hat! Cape St. James, located at the south end of Haida Gwaii, British Columbia, is Cana-da's windiest place. It sees more days with gale-force winds than anywhere else in the nation.

Cold summer cities

It could claim the title of "bad summer capital of Canada." St. John's has the nation's lowest average daily summer temperature (at just 13.9°C) and the fewest hot days (an average of only 0.2 days during June, July and August when the temperature exceeds 30°C). Vancouver could be considered a close second for that ominous title. It has a daily average summer temperature of 16.8°C and 0.2 days of summer temperatures over 30°C.

Freezing cities in summer

Yes, it happens. Below zero temperatures in summer — yes, summer — in large Canadian cities. Here are the seven cities across the country that have seen the freezing mark in June, July or August:

City	°C	Date
Regina, SK	−5.6	June 12, 1969
Calgary, AB	−3.3	June 8, 1891
Winnipeg, MB	−3.3	June 3, 1964
Saguenay, SK	−3.3	June 10, 1968
Saskatoon, SK	−2.8	August 23, 1901
Sherbrooke, QC	−2.2	June 3, 1965
St. John's, NL	−1.1	July 5, 1976

Driest city

Conserve the water. Medicine Hat, Alberta, has more dry days than any other Canadian city, with 271 days per year without measurable precipitation.

Driest year

The driest year ever recorded in Canada occurred in 1949 at Arctic Bay, Northwest Territories, where only 12.7 ml of precipitation fell.

Most rain in 1 hour

The greatest recorded rainfall over the span of 1 hour in Canada occurred on May 31, 1961, at Buffalo Gap, Saskatchewan. A total of 254 ml (10 inches) of rain fell between 4:30 p.m and 5:30 p.m.

Largest single-day downpours in Canada

Date	Place	inches	ml
October 6, 1967	Ucluelet, BC	19.3	489.2
January 26, 1984	McInnes Island, BC	12.6	319
January 14, 1961	Seymour Falls, BC	12.4	314
November 14, 1991	Mitchell Inlet, BC	12.1	306
November 11, 1990	Tahsis, BC	11.8	300
November 10, 1990	Seymour Falls, BC	11.8	300

Wettest places outside of BC

The rest of Canada hardly compares to British Columbia when it comes to annual precipitation averages. The next wettest community receives 79 fewer rainy days and more than 600 ml less precipitation. Here are the nation's other wettest places:

Average annual precipitation

Days (0.2 mm)	Place	inches	ml
164	Wreck Cove, NS	76.6	1,946
183	Red Harbour, NL	72.5	1,841
147	Pool's Cove, NL	72.0	1,828
154	Guysborough, NS	71.4	1,815
219	Forêt Montmorency, QC	62.3	1,583
236	Saint-Fortunat, QC	60.7	1,542
172	Alma, NB	59.5	1,510
163	Allenford, ON	50.9	1,294
175	New Glasgow, PEI	49.5	1,258
149	Blyth, ON	49.1	1,247
162	Waterton Village, AB	43.2	1,096

Wettest spot

Bring an umbrella. Mitchell Inlet on British Columbia's Haida Gwaii Island is Canada's wettest place. It receives 6,325 ml of precipitation each year, of which 99 percent is rain. That's more than 6 m annually!

Wettest city

Bring an umbrella. Prince Rupert, British Columbia, is Canada's wettest city. It gets an average of 2,619 ml of precipitation every year.

Wettest Canadian lightstation

Boat Bluff lightstation, on the south end of Sarah Island, British Columbia, registers 5,047 ml of precipitation annually, most of which is rain.

Most consecutive rainy days

Vancouver claims the record among large Canadian cities (those with a population of 100,000 and greater) for the most consecutive days of rain: 29, in 1953, from January 6 to February 3. The city nearly broke the record in January 2006, after 23 straight days of rain.

Most lightning

Flash! The north shore of Lake Erie near Highgate, Ontario, gets the greatest annual number of days (50 in 2006) with lightning of any inland place in Canada.

Rain in the rainiest province

British Columbia certainly lives up to its reputation as a rainy province. Here's a chart showing the average annual precipitation, most of which is rain, for the province's wettest communities.

Days (0.2 mm)	Place	inches	ml
275	Mitchell Inlet	385.9	6,325
203	Hartley Bay	179.0	4,548
269	Tahsis	169.5	4,305
207	Port Renfrew	138.0	3,505
225	Port Alice	134.9	3,427
206	Ucluelet	131.9	3,351
208	Tofino	128.8	3,271
243	Prince Rupert	103.1	2,619

Northernmost lightning

The farthest north a lightning flash was detected in Canada was over Viscount Melville Sound, northwest of Prince of Wales Island, on August 11, 2013.

Most lightning for a city

Call it Canada's lightning capital. Windsor, Ontario, is the Canadian city that had the most lightning in any one year: 47 days with lightning in 2006.

First billion-dollar disaster

The storm's moniker has a nice ring to it, but there was nothing nice about the disaster. The first billion-dollar disaster in Canadian history was the flood that hit Saguenay, Quebec, from July 18 to 21, 1996. Roads and bridges throughout the area were destroyed, close to 500 homes were destroyed, 16,000 residents were evacuated and 10 people were killed.

Weather

Longest growing seasons

Canadian cities with the longest growing seasons based on the average number of frost-free days:

City	Days
Vancouver, BC	237
Victoria, BC	211
Abbotsford, BC	208
Toronto, ON	203
Windsor, ON	195
Halifax, NS	182
St. Catharines, ON	179
Hamilton, ON	177
Oshawa, ON	168
Peterborough, ON	168

Highest average temperature

Canada's West Coast is well known for being rainy, but not for being hot. Still, you could consider Victoria Canada's hottest major city. It has the country's highest recorded average daily maximum temperature at 15.3°C. Victoria also has the hottest recorded nights, with an average daily minimum temperature of 7.1°C.

Cities with the highest average temperatures

City	High °F	High °C
Victoria, BC	60	15.3
Abbotsford, BC	59	15.1
Kelowna, BC	59	14.7
Windsor, ON	58	14.4
Vancouver, BC	57	13.9
St. Catharines, ON	56	13.6
Brantford, ON	56	13.2
Hamilton, ON	56	13.1
Toronto, ON	55	12.9
London, ON	55	12.7
Oshawa, ON	54	12.1

Hottest cities at night

The country's hottest cities at night, based on average daily minimum temperature annually:

City	Low °F	Low °C
Victoria, BC	45	7.1
Vancouver, BC	44	6.8
Toronto, ON	43	5.9
Abbotsford, BC	42	5.8
Windsor, ON	42	5.4
St. Catharines, ON	40	4.4
Kelowna, BC	39	4.1
Oshawa, ON	39	4.1
Hamilton, ON	39	4.0
Halifax, NS	38	3.6

Hottest year

The hottest year: 1998. Canada recorded its second-warmest winter and warmest spring, summer and fall. Temperatures that year were an average 2.4°C higher than typical.

Hot day in Saskatchewan

On July 5, 1937, the mercury soared to 45°C in Yellow Grass, Saskatchewan.

Temperatures higher than 40°C

Here's a list of when and where temperatures 40°C and higher were recorded in Canada:

Location	°C	Date(s)
Midale and Yellow Grass, SK	45.0	July 5, 1937
Lillooet and Lytton, BC	44.4	July 16 & 17, 1941
Emerson, MB	44.4	July 12, 1936
St. Albans, MB	44.4	July 11, 1936
Fort Macleod, AB	43.3	July 18, 1941
Regina, SK	43.3	July 5, 1937
Brandon and Morden, MB	43.3	July 11, 1936
Osoyoos, BC	42.8	July 17, 1998
Oliver, BC	42.8	July 27, 1939
Spences Bridge, BC	42.5	July 23, 1994
Atikokan, ON	42.2	July 11 & 12, 1936
Medicine Hat, AB	42.2	July 12, 1886
Moose Jaw, SK	41.7	August 6, 1949
Northwest River, NL	41.7	August 11, 1914
Saskatoon, SK	40.6	June 5, 1988
Kamloops, BC	40.6	July 31, 1971
Winnipeg, MB	40.6	August 7, 1949
Toronto, ON	40.6	July 10, 1936
Windsor, ON	40.2	June 25, 1988
Temiscamingue, QC	40.0	July 6, 1921

The hottest and the coldest

As most Canadians know and have experienced, this country can deliver a wide range of temperatures, from cold winter nights to hot summer days. Interestingly, among Canada's large cities, Regina lays claim to both the country's lowest recorded temperature and its highest. The city sweltered at 43.3°C on July 5, 1937. Likewise, Winnipeg and Saskatoon, both holding cold-weather records themselves, also posted some of the highest recorded temperatures for large Canadian cities; they tied for second place at 40.6°C (Winnipeg on August 7, 1949, and Saskatoon on June 5, 1988).

Deadliest heat wave

Environment Canada calls it the deadliest heat wave in history. From July 5 to 17, 1936, temperatures in Manitoba and Ontario were more than 44°C and responsible for the death of 1,180 people (largely infants and the elderly). In an unfortunate twist of fate, 400 of those deaths were attributed to drowning from people trying to escape the heat. It was so hot that steel railways and bridge girders twisted and crops dried up.

▶▶ Weather

Most sunshine ever

"Get out the suntan lotion" isn't a commonly heard refrain in Canada's Far North. But the most sunshine any community in Canada ever observed in one month was 621 hours in Eureka, Ellesmere Island, Northwest Territories (now Nunavut), during May 1973.

Most hours of sunshine

Despite the fact they're some of the country's snowiest and coldest cities, the following cities are also the sunniest. Here's the list of the cities that receive the highest average hours of sunlight annually:

City	Hours
Calgary, AB	2,396
Winnipeg, MB	2,353
Edmonton, AB	2,345
Regina, SK	2,318
Saskatoon, SK	2,268
Thunder Bay, ON	2,121
Hamilton, ON	2,111
Victoria, BC	2,109
Ottawa, ON	2,084
Toronto, ON	2,066

Most days of sunshine

Here's the nation's top 10 sunniest cities, as measured by average days where the sun shines brightly enough to be measured:

City	Days
Calgary, AB	333
Edmonton, AB	325
Regina, SK	322
Saskatoon, SK	319
Winnipeg, MB	316
Victoria, BC	308
Montreal, QC	305
Toronto, ON	305
Thunder Bay, ON	305
Kelowna, BC	304

Percentage of sunshine

Here's a list of the country's sunniest cities, as measured by percentage of daylight hours that the sun shines on average:

City	Sunshine (%)
Calgary, AB	52
Winnipeg, MB	51
Edmonton, AB	50
Regina, SK	50
Saskatoon, SK	49
Thunder Bay, ON	46
Hamilton, ON	45
Ottawa, ON	45
Toronto, ON	44
Montreal, QC	44

Sunshine capital

Although it's a smaller community than Calgary, Estevan, in southeast Saskatchewan, is Canada's sunshine capital. It averages 2,404 hours of sunlight each year over 324 days.

Sunniest big city

Looking for a staycation suntan? Move to Calgary. It is the nation's sunniest large city, getting 2,396 hours of sunshine on average annually. And it comes over 333 days. That's more than half of the city's daylight hours.

Warming country

All of Canada has become warmer since the mid-20th century. Between 1948 and 2016, the nation's average temperature rose by 1.7°C, about double the global rate. The average annual temperature in Canada north of 60° latitude have risen by 2.3°C.

Fastest-rising temperatures

Need proof that climate change is a problem? Average winter temperatures in Yukon and northern British Columbia went up by 4.9°C between 1948 and 2007 — the fastest-rising temperatures in the country.

No change in fall temperatures

Two parts of the country have bucked the warming trend. During autumn in the extreme south of Ontario and Quebec, the average temperature has not changed since 1948.

Provinces getting colder

Other places in Canada have also seen average seasonal temperatures that don't follow the overall warming trend. Since 1948, the Atlantic provinces have grown colder in winter, and in the months of September, October and November, average temperatures decreased in Alberta, Saskatchewan, Manitoba, Yukon and northern British Columbia.

Curious about climate change?

The Prairie Climate Centre at the University of Winnipeg has created an interactive tool called the Climate Atlas of Canada. It combines climate science, mapping, videography and storytelling to help people better understand the issue of climate change and provides tools and solutions that everyone can try.

Disaster!

Famous shipwreck

Immortalized in singer Gordon Lightfoot's song "The Wreck of the Edmund Fitzgerald," a severe storm on November 10, 1975 — accompanied by 20 m high waves on Lake Superior — sank the largest bulk ore carrier on the Great Lakes, the SS *Edmund Fitzgerald*. The ship's crew of 29 was lost.

Empress of Ireland

The worst maritime disaster in Canadian history was the sinking of the SS *Empress of Ireland* in the St. Lawrence River near Rimouski, Quebec, on May 29, 1914. A total of 1,014 people died when the ship collided with the Norwegian collier *Storstad* in the fog.

Worst encounter with an iceberg

The world's worst iceberg accident? The reportedly "unsinkable" *Titanic* hit an iceberg on April 14, 1912, 700 km southeast of Newfoundland, and 1,500 people died in the waters of the north Atlantic. The disaster is considered one of the planet's worst maritime disasters ever.

Worst rockslide

The worst rockslide in Canadian history occurred on April 29, 1903, when 82 million tonnes of rock crashed down from Turtle Mountain on the town of Frank, Alberta. The slide killed 70 people.

Worst streetcar disaster

The worst streetcar disaster in North America occurred on May 26, 1896, when a car plunged into the Victoria Harbour after a span fell out of the bridge at Point Ellice. Fifty-five people died.

Halifax Explosion

The world's largest accidental explosion (and Canada's worst disaster) was the Halifax Explosion of December 6, 1917. Some 1,600 people were killed, another 9,000 injured and 6,000 left homeless in the disaster, caused when the French munitions carrier *Mont Blanc* and the Belgian relief vessel *Imo* collided in the harbour's Narrows.

Worst epidemic

Canada's worst epidemic? Spanish influenza, brought home in 1918 by soldiers returning from the First World War. The Spanish flu killed some 50,000 Canadians. Worldwide, it's believed to have claimed the lives of more people than the Great War itself.

Coronavirus

On January 9, 2020, the world's first fatality from the novel coronavirus (later also known as COVID-19) was reported in Wuhan, China. The virus spread rapidly across China and then Europe, eventually hitting Canada on January 25. By March 11, the World Health Organization had declared COVID-19 a worldwide pandemic. That announcement triggered worldwide shutdowns of schools and stores and made terms like "social distancing" commonplace in Canadian homes. As of publication, Canada has reported more than 90,000 cases and 7,500 deaths.

▶▶ *Disaster!*

Deadliest earthquake

The deadliest recorded earthquake in Canadian history claimed 27 lives, all of whom drowned in the resulting tsunami that hit Newfoundland's Burin Pennisula. Centred near the Laurentian slope, offshore between Newfoundland and Nova Scotia, the 7.2-magnitude quake struck on November 18, 1929.

Rogers Pass avalanche

The deadliest avalanche in Canadian history occurred on March 5, 1910, when 58 railway workers were killed 2 km west of Rogers Pass, British Columbia. Their engine was hit by a snow slide and hurtled 500 m into Bear Creek. More than 600 volunteers dug through 10 m of snow with shovels and pickaxes in search of survivors.

Deadliest tornado

Known as "the Regina Cyclone," the tornado that hit Saskatchewan's capital in the late afternoon of June 30, 1912, is considered the deadliest such storm in Canadian history. The whirlwind tore through six city blocks, killed 28 people and injured 300 more. It destroyed 500 buildings and left a quarter of the city's population homeless. It took an estimated 40 years to pay for the damages.

Worst flood

The Red River Flood in the spring of 1950 is considered the worst flood disaster in Canadian history. The river crested 9.2 m above its normal level in Winnipeg. Just one person drowned, but the flood forced the evacuation of 100,000 people from southern Manitoba, damaged 5,000 homes and buildings, and cost $550 million in property damage. Following the disaster, the provincial government decided to build the Winnipeg Floodway to mitigate future flooding.

Deadliest sinkhole

The deadliest recorded sinkhole in Canada happened on May 4, 1971, when heavy rain created a sinkhole 600 m wide and 30 m deep in Saint-Jean-Vianney, Quebec. The hole and associated mudslide claimed the lives of 31 people and swallowed 35 homes, a bus and several cars.

Deadliest train wreck

Canada's deadliest train disaster occurred on June 29, 1864, near St-Hilaire, Quebec, on the Grand Trunk Railway. It's believed 99 passengers were killed and another 100 injured when the train — carrying 458 people, largely German and Polish immigrants — plunged into the Richelieu River after failing to stop for an open swing bridge.

32 ▶ O'Canada!
(D'oh Canada!)

The apology act

Sorry to break it to you, but Canadians are so polite that the government had to enact a law that specifies that if a Canadian apologizes, it is not an expression of guilt. That's right — Canadians use the word *sorry* so much that they feared it would be used against them in court. Did someone bump into you while walking down the road? Feel free to apologize like a true Canadian without worrying that you will be held liable for any injuries that came from the collision — whether you were at — fault or not. To Canadians, apologizing is a way of life, and in order to be free with the word, they created a law, Bill 108 (Apology Act of 2009), to protect their right to use it as frequently as they want.

Second-largest country

Canada is the second-largest country in the world, but it has only 0.5 percent of the world's population.

National phone number

Did you know that our nation has its own phone number? Yep, it's 1-800-O-Canada. Call that number to find out anything want to know about moving to, or living and working in, Canada.

Less gravity

One particular part of Canada has puzzled scientists for over 40 years: the Hudson Bay area appears to have less gravity than the rest of the world. In fact, residents in the region (including some parts of Quebec) weigh one-tenth of an ounce less than their counterparts weigh elsewhere around the world.

Lots of garbage

Here's a dirty secret. Canada produces nearly 673 kg of waste, per person, each year — and we aren't managing it that well, as only 20 percent of our waste gets recycled. The lion's share of our garbage goes to landfill. Of the 36 member countries of the Organization for Economic Co-operation and Development (OECD), Canada is the eighth most waste-producing nation. Only three countries create more waste than Canada on a per capita basis: the United States, Denmark and New Zealand.

Most energy users

Also according to a 2013 report from the Conference Board of Canada (How Canada Performs — Environment), Canadians are the largest users of energy in the developed world.

The "eh" word

Did you now the word *eh* is officially in the *Canadian Oxford Dictionary*?

it's a CANADIAN thing eh?

▶▶ *O'Canada! (D'oh Canada!)*

Milk in a bag

It wasn't too long ago that households around the country had milk delivered in glass bottles by a milkman, similar to in the United States and the United Kingdom — at least up until 1967, when the country was preparing to make the switch to the metric system. DuPont, the Canadian packaging company, teamed up with Guaranteed Pure Milk Company to create new packaging to fit the new mandated units. Rather than redesigning glass bottles and plastic jugs, the collaboration spawned the development of the polyethylene milk bag that is still used today. Not only did it allow for more accurate measurements, but it was easier and more cost-effective to transport. Approximately 80 percent of the milk sold in Canada is in bags. Although the trend never did catch on in the United States (with the exception of Minnesota and Wisconsin), other countries such as India, Russia, South Africa, Argentina, Uruguay, Hungary and China have all adopted use of the ever-practical milk-in-a-bag.

Highest food prices

In Nunavut, a carton of orange juice can cost $14 and a head of cabbage, $28. Those who live in Canada's North, particularly in Nunavut, can expect to pay as much as three times the national average in food prices. There are no roads or rail into the territory — it is accessible only by ship or plane (and the weather can dictate delays on any given day) so it costs a lot more to transport food into the territory.

Most salt

That's salty. Canada has the world's largest per capita use of salt. It's estimated that each Canadian uses more than 360 kg of salt annually. Salt as a de-icing agent makes up a large part of this figure.

Smarties

Just one question: "When you eat your Smarties, do you eat the red ones last?"
Well, no matter which way you eat them, you won't find Smarties in the United States. In fact, the chalky candy-flavoured tablets known affectionately as "Rockets" to Canadians is what Americans call Smarties. That's because Smarties, the traditional candy-coated chocolate treat, aren't sold in the United States. Smarties were invented in 1937 and made by Rowntree's until 1988, when Rowntree's was acquired by Nestlé. They are now a Nestlé brand worldwide.

Most donut shops

It goes without saying that the country that brought the world Tim Hortons would also have the most donut shops per capita. In fact, just counting Tims locations alone, there's roughly one location for every 8,800 people!

Ketchup chips

Hostess Potato Chips (now Lay's) is credited with inventing ketchup chips in the 1970s. The company experimented with a tomato-flavoured chip and (behold!) the ketchup chip was born. While Americans are just now warming up to this flavour, it is still rare to find this snack on store shelves in the United States. Lay's ketchup chips, considered by many the premier brand for this flavour anomaly, can only be found in Canada.

Most mac and cheese

Not a joke: Canadians love macaroni and cheese ... I mean really love it. In fact, they are such huge fans of the meal, they gave it its own day — July 14 is National Mac and Cheese Day in Canada. Kraft Dinner (the ubiquitous boxed mac and cheese) is so beloved by Canadians it is the most popular food item sold in grocery stores around the nation. Of the 7 million boxes sold per week around the world, Canadians purchase 1.7 million.

Hawaiian pizza

Nothing says Hawaii like the shores of Lake Erie, right? Well, it was against that backdrop in 1962 that Sam Panopoulos decided to put pineapple on pizza in his Chatham-area restaurant. He called it "Hawaiian" after the brand of canned pineapple he used on the pizza.

▶▶ O'Canada! (D'oh Canada!)

Most creme eggs

In a sickeningly-sweet feat of eating, competitive eater Peter Czerwinski gobbled six Cadbury Creme Eggs in one minute. Think you can do it faster? If so, tell Guinness World Records!

Most toenails

Ever wonder who's got the largest collection of toenails? Well, look no further than the Atlantic Partnership for Tomorrow's Health (Atlantic PATH). The research organization collected clippings from 24,999 individuals during a research project aimed at better understanding cancer and chronic disease. It turns out that toenails can hold vital data from our diets and environmental exposures.

Sour toe?

It's as weird as it is true. Adults who visit the Sourdough Saloon in Dawson City, Yukon, can join the Sourtoe Cocktail Club. To become a member all a person has to do is finish a drink (of anything) that also includes a mummified human toe! You don't drink the toe (that's gross!), but as the motto says: "You can drink it fast, you can drink it slow, but your lips must touch that gnarly toe..."

Poo emoji

Here's a stinker — Canada on the whole uses the poo emoji more frequently than any other any other country. Pyeww!

Santa Claus is Canadian

In 2010, Immigration Minister Jason Kenney reaffirmed that Santa Claus is, indeed, a Canadian citizen. The jolly elf even appeared at a special swearing-in ceremony for 100 new Canadians on December 22. "We wish Mr. Claus all the best in his Christmas Eve duties again this year," said Minister Kenney. "And rest assured, as a Canadian citizen living in Canada's North, he can re-enter Canada freely once his trip around the world is complete."

Most Santa

Canadian Jean-Guy Laquerre has more than 25,000 different items of Santa Claus memorabilia — the most in the world as recognized by Guinness World Records. His collection includes 2,360 figurines, 2,846 cards and postcards from 33 countries, 1,312 serviettes and 241 pins and brooches.

O'Canada! (D'oh Canada!)

Most-visited nation that's not the United States

Do you know the most popular destination for Canadians outside of the United States? Mexico. Canadians made nearly 1.7 million visits there in 2018, according to Statistics Canada.

Second most-visited nation that's not the United States

The second most-visited nation by Canadians that's not America? Cuba, where Canadians made 895,000 overnight visits in 2018, according to Statistics Canada. The United Kingdom followed, with Canadians making 748,000 overnight visits in 2018.

Our own *Simpsons* episode

Speaking of travel, in season 30 episode 21 (titled "D'oh Canada"), Homer and the gang travel to Niagara Falls and Lisa accidentally winds up on the Canadian side. Once there she falls in love with America's northern neighbour (she's especially pleased with free health care and Canadian science text books that acknowledge climate change). However, the episode wasn't without scandal. The show provided blunt commentary on seal hunting, and many Newfoundlanders voiced displeasure with how they were portrayed.

Canada's favourite American states

Canadians aren't shy about visiting our neighbours to the south. But do you know which American state is most visited by Canadians, according to Statistics Canada? Florida saw 4.1 million overnight visits from Canadians in 2018. New York State was second with 3.1 million visits, while Washington State was third with 2.5 million.

Pop Culture | **Music**

No. 1 country

Canadian country music sweetheart Shania Twain, born in Windsor, Ontario, on August 28, 1965, left her mark on the genre. Twain's third album, *Come on Over* (1997), holds the record for most weeks at No. 1 on Billboard's country album chart. It spent 50 weeks at the top , eclipsing her 1995 release, *The Woman in Me*, which spent 29 weeks at the top. With 40 million copies sold, *Come on Over* is the biggest-selling studio album by a female solo artist. It is a 20-times Platinum record in the United States and is the biggest-selling album of country music in America by a solo artist.

Most Hot 100

In 2020, Canadian rapper Drake, born on October 24, 1986, in Toronto, became the artist with the most songs ever charted on the Billboard Hot 100. He scored the feat with his song "Oprah's Bank Account," which debuted at No. 89, becoming his 208th title on the chart. The previous record holder was the cast of the television show *Glee*, which had 207 entries.

DRAKE

Five No. 1 hits

You're likely very familiar with Justin Bieber. Born in Stratford, Ontario, on March 1, 1994, Bieber became the first musician with five No. 1 albums on the Billboard 200 chart before he was 19 years old. He achieved the feat in early 2013 with his *Believe Acoustic* album. His previous No. 1 albums are *Believe* (2012), *Under the Mistletoe* (2011), *Never Say Never: The Remixes* (2011) and *My World 2.0* (2010).

JUSTIN BIEBER

One million records

Singer-songwriter Bryan Adams, born in Kingston, Ontario, on November 5, 1959, was the first Canadian musician to sell one million albums in Canada, for his 1984 album, *Reckless*.

First Canadian woman to top American charts

Musician Alanis Morissette, born in Ottawa on June 1, 1974, is the first Canadian woman to have a Billboard No. 1 album with her 1995 release, *Jagged Little Pill*. It won four Grammys, including Album of the Year, and has sold more than 33 million copies.

Most top 10 songs in one year

In 2018 Drake dethroned the Beatles as the artist with the most Top Ten songs on Billboard's Hot 100 chart in a single year when his song "MIA," a collaboration with Puerto Rican singer Bad Bunny, reached number 5 on the list — Drake's 12th single to reach the Top Ten list that year. By his 32nd birthday, Drake had had 32 Top Ten songs on the Billboard Hot 100 chart — more than any other solo male artist.

Canadian chart toppers

The year 2015 was an exceptionally good one for Canadian musicians. That year, Canadians ruled the pop charts, snagging the top four spots on the Billboard charts. The Weeknd's "Earned It" soared to the No. 3 spot in May 2015, spending 18 weeks on the Billboard Top Ten list, and he released his hit song "I Can't Feel My Face," which soared to the No. 1 spot on the Billboard charts in August, with 19 weeks in the Top Ten; Drake's "Hotline Bling" took the No. 2 spot for one week in October; Justin Bieber's song "What Do You Mean" became the singer's first single to reach the top of the Billboard Hot 100, reaching No. 1 in September and spending 21 weeks in the Top Ten; and Shawn Mendes' single "Stitches" made it to No. 4 on the Billboard Hot 100, with 18 weeks in the Top Ten.

Most downloaded tracks

Three No. 1 albums

Born in Belleville, Ontario, on September 27, 1984, singer-songwriter Avril Lavigne has already racked up many achievements:

▶ Her song "Girlfriend" was the most downloaded track worldwide in 2007, according to the International Federation of the Phonographic Industry.

▶ Her album *Let Go* is one of the rare albums by a Canadian to attain Diamond certification in Canada.

▶ She is the second artist to have three number one songs from a debut album on Billboard's Mainstream Top 40 list.

▶ In 2019, Avril Lavigne was the 11th bestselling female singer of the decade in the United States, selling over 16 million albums by 2015 alone.

Good things happen in threes, and in musician Shawn Mendes' case, the number three may just be his lucky number. In 2018, Mendes' self-titled third album made him the third-youngest solo artist to have three number one albums on the Billboard 200 chart. Born in Pickering, Ontario, Mendes has seen many milestones since his debut album in 2015, including being one of only 11 solo artists to have an album hit number one on the charts before turning 16 years old.

First Canadian Best New Artist winner

In 2018, singer-songwriter Alessia Cara, born July 11, 1996, in Brampton, Ontario, cemented her place in music history by becoming the first-ever Canadian to win the highly sought after Best New Artist Grammy Award.

First French gold record

One of the many accomplishments of famed songstress Céline Dion, born March 30, 1968, in Charlemagne, Quebec: she was the first Canadian to receive a Gold record in France. She managed the feat in 1983 at just 15 years old.

Mr. Grammy

Watching events such as the Grammy Awards on live television is second nature these days. But when television producer Pierre Cossette, born in Valleyfield, Quebec, on December 15, 1923, first suggested the idea in 1970, he had a tough job convincing American network executives. Cossette, now known as "Mr. Grammy," was executive producer of the show for 35 years before he retired.

First No. 1 hit

Guess who was the first Canadian-based band to have a No. 1 hit in the United States? The question's the answer. "American Woman" by the Guess Who, based in Winnipeg, Manitoba, hit the top of the Billboard Hot 100 list the weeks of May 9, 16 and 23 in 1970.

The truest and most human story of the Great White Snows

A picture with more drama, greater thrill, and stronger action than any picture you ever saw.

REVILLON FRÈRES PRESENT

NANOOK OF THE NORTH

A STORY OF LIFE AND LOVE IN THE ACTUAL ARCTIC

PRODUCED BY ROBERT J. FLAHERTY, F.R.G.S.

Pathépicture

First documentary

Nanook of the North, a silent movie from 1922 about a group of Inuit living on the coast of Hudson Bay, is widely regarded as the first full-length documentary film.

Oscars for Canadian siblings

Here's a unique Canadian milestone from the Oscars: brother and sister (and natives of Quebec) Douglas and Norma Shearer were the first siblings to ever win Academy Awards in the same year. In 1931, Douglas took the Oscar for Best Sound Recording for *The Big House*, while Norma captured Best Actress for her role in *The Divorcee*.

Canadian *Saturday Night Live*

While the rumours of his being the inspiration for Dr. Evil of *Austin Powers* fame have been denied, there's no question television producer Lorne Michaels is a mad genius. Born in Toronto on November 17, 1944, Michaels' most noteworthy accomplishment is as the creator and executive producer of *Saturday Night Live*, the longest-running and highest-rated late-night television show ever.

Sandra Oh's triple feat

On January 5, 2019, Ottawa's Sandra Oh made history as the first person of Asian descent to host the Golden Globe Awards. Her win for best actress that night for her role in *Killing Eve* also made her the first woman of Asian descent to win multiple Golden Globes (her first coming in 2005 for her work on *Grey's Anatomy*) and the first woman of Asian descent in 39 years to win the Golden Globe for best actress in a TV drama.

First stars in cement

Early Hollywood actress Mary Pickford, and her husband at the time, Douglas Fairbanks, were the first stars to cast their hands and feet in cement in front of the Grauman's Chinese Theatre in Hollywood, on April 30, 1927. Known as "America's sweetheart," Pickford was born in Toronto on April 8, 1892.

Highest grossing movies

Talk about Hollywood North! James Cameron, born in Kapuskasing, Ontario, is the writer and director of two of the highest-grossing movies of all time, *Avatar* (2009) and *Titanic* (1997). The two films combined have grossed $5 billion, with *Avatar*, at $2.8 billion, besting *Titanic* at $2.2 billion. In 2020, *Avengers: Endgame* narrowly took the No. 1 spot from *Avatar*.

Canadian Warner Bros.

How's this for a Canadian connection to Hollywood royalty? Along with his brothers Henry M., Albert and Sam, Jack L. Warner, who was born in London, Ontario, on August 2, 1892, founded Warner Bros. Pictures Inc., the massive Hollywood film studio, in 1923. Jack became one of the most famous and significant film executives of early Hollywood.

Fourth-youngest Best Actress Oscar nominee

Ellen Page, born in Halifax, Nova Scotia, in 1987, became the fourth-youngest woman to receive a Best Actress Academy Award nomination in 2008 at the age of 20 years old for her role in the film *Juno*.

Oldest Oscar winner

Who says you can't teach an old dog new tricks? Canadian actor Christopher Plummer, born in Toronto on December 13, 1929, is the oldest actor to ever win an Oscar. Plummer captured the 2012 Academy Award for Best Supporting Actor for his role in *Beginners* at the age of 82.

Second-youngest Best Actress Oscar winner

Anna Paquin is the second-youngest Best Actress Oscar winner, but did you know she is a Canadian? Paquin was born in Winnipeg, Manitoba, in 1982.

Double Best Actor nominee

London, Ontario, native Ryan Gosling may have started out on the Disney Channel's *The Mickey Mouse Club*, but nowadays Gosling is known for his roles in critically acclaimed movies such as the musical drama *La La Land*, for which he received his second Best Actor Academy Award nomination in 2017, making him one of only three Canadians who have been nominated for the Best Actor Academy Award twice. Gosling scored his first Best Actor Oscar nod in 2006 for his role in *Half Nelson*.

Longest-running drama series

The Degrassi franchise is synonymous with Canada, particularly as it is the country's longest-running television drama series. The show was initially released in 1980 as several stand-alone after-school specials produced by Kit Hood and Linda Schuyler, a teacher who wanted to showcase issues that children struggle with daily. The specials were so successful that in 1987, the spin-off *Degrassi Junior High* aired, featuring some of the same actors from the children's series navigating the world of junior high school. Since then, the Degrassi series has aired on and off for over 35 years, giving rise to iconic entertainers such as rapper Drake and actress Nina Dobrev of *The Vampire Diaries* fame.

The Arts

First symphony
The Quebec Symphony Orchestra, based in Quebec City, is the oldest symphony in Canada. It was officially formed on October 3, 1902, and gave its first performance on November 28 that year. Today, the orchestra attracts an audience of about 100,000 annually.

First orchestra concert for children
In 1924–25, its second season, the Toronto Symphony Orchestra performed the first orchestra concert specifically for children. The performance was part of the orchestra's efforts to engage and attract a younger audience.

260

Oldest ballet company

The Royal Winnipeg Ballet is the nation's oldest dance company and the second oldest in North America. Founded as the Winnipeg Ballet Club by Gweneth Lloyd and Betty Farrally, the organization gave its first performance in 1939. The club received a royal charter from Queen Elizabeth II in 1953 to become the first "Royal" ballet company of the Commonwealth.

First National Ballet *Giselle*

The National Ballet of Canada (NBC) was formed in 1951. Its first performance was *Giselle* (considered the *Hamlet* of dance) on November 12 of that year at Toronto's Eaton Auditorium. The ballet has been performed many times since then by the NBC, which is one of the few ballet companies that has always had its own orchestra.

Largest opera company

The Canadian Opera Company was the nation's first opera company, and it is the largest. It began as the Canadian Opera Festival in February 1950, and today the COC attracts about 140,000 patrons each season.

Largest classical theatre

Stratford, Ontario, hosts the largest classical repertory theatre in North America. Founded in 1953, the Stratford Festival presents numerous shows spring through fall annually at four theatres in the town. In 2013, the festival attracted 480,000 patrons.

Best new musical

Come from Away, a musical depicting the story of American passengers stranded in Gander, Newfoundland, during the September 11, 2001 attacks, is only the fifth Canadian musical to make it to Broadway. Originally produced as a Sheridan College Theatre Production by Irene Sankoff and David Hein, *Come from Away* has gone on to win numerous awards, including a Tony Award for Direction of a Musical, and it is now the first Canadian production to win the London, England, Laurence Olivier Award for Best New Musical.

Last double-decker theatre

Toronto's Elgin and Winter Garden Theatre Centre is the last operating double-decker theatre (two separate and distinctive theatres stacked on top of one another) on the planet. It is also considered one of the most beautiful theatre complexes in the world. The complex was built in 1913 as the flagship of Marcus Loew's theatre chain.

First opera and ballet theatre

One of a kind: the Four Seasons Centre for the Performing Arts in Toronto was the first theatre in Canada built specifically for opera and ballet performances. Opened in 2006, the facility features a modern take on the traditional horse-shoe-shaped auditorium, which delivers great sightlines and acoustics. The building is the permanent home of the Canadian Opera Company and the National Ballet of Canada.

Most expensive art

During his life, Toronto painter Alex Colville, who died on July 16, 2013, at the age of 92, held the record for the highest price paid for a work of art by a living Canadian artist. "Man on Verandah," painted in 1953, was purchased at an auction on November 25, 2010, for $1.287 million.

The most laughs

Its mission statement is simple: "Make people happy." The annual Just for Laughs comedy festival in Montreal is the world's largest, with audiences of nearly two million people each July. The Montreal festival has grown into a major comedy business operation, with festivals in Toronto, Chicago and Sydney, Australia; television shows (*Gags*, seen in 135 countries); live tours and talent management.

First Booker

Author Michael Ondaatje was the first Canadian to win the Man Booker Prize, a £50,000 literary award for the best novel of the year written by a citizen of the United Kingdom, the Commonwealth or the Republic of Ireland. Ondaatje and his novel *The English Patient* shared the 1992 Booker with Barry Unsworth and his work *Sacred Hunger*.

Best Canadian cartoonist

Jeff Lemire is not only an award-winning author, Lemire, from Essex County, Ontario, has a long career writing for comic books such as *Superboy* and *Justice League*. He currently writes for the DC comics *Green Arrow* and *Justice League United*. In 2009 and 2013, Lemire won the Shuster Award for Best Canadian Cartoonist.

Canadian Superman

Superman — created by Canadian artist Joe Shuster and American, Jerome Siegel — made his first appearance in the June 1938 issue of *Action Comics*, a comic book publisher created by Shuster and Siegel in 1938.

Bestselling book

Lucy Maud Montgomery's iconic novel *Anne of Green Gables* has sold over 50 million copies in over 36 languages, making it one of the bestselling novels worldwide. Within months of its original publication, the book sold over 19,000 copies. Since then, it has been adapted into various films, countless animated and live action TV specials, plays and musicals.

First animated Spider-Man

Don't look now, but it's your friendly *Canadian* neighborhood Spider-Man! Yes, you heard right — the original animated Spider-Man series was produced with a cast comprised of mostly Canadian actors. In fact, Toronto, Ontario, actor Paul Soles was the voice of Spider-Man in the original series from 1967 to 1970.

Most Governor General's Literary Awards

Looking for Governor General–approved literature? Look no further than the work of author Hugh MacLennan or Michael Ondaatje. Each has won more Governor General Literary Awards than anyone else: a total of five each. First presented in 1936, the first recipients of these prestigious awards were Bertram Brooker (fiction), for his book *Think of the Earth*, and T.B. Roberton (non-fiction), for a series of newspaper pieces.

King of kid-lit

Quick: name the bestselling children's book author of all time. Did you know it is Canada's "King of Kid-Lit," Robert Munsch? Munsch, who lives in Guelph, Ontario, has penned more than 40 books, and his most famous title, *Love You Forever*, has sold more than 30 million copies.

▶▶ *Pop Culture*
Video & Gaming

First female late-night TV host

Letterman, Leno, Kimmel, Fallon, and now ... Lilly Singh. Yes, YouTube star and comedian Singh — born in Scarborough, Ontario, on September 26, 1988 — enters the historic hallways of late-night television as the first woman to host a late-night talk show on a major television network. *A Little Late with Lilly Singh* premiered on NBC in September 2019.

First video-game franchise

Did you know that the popular video game *Assassin's Creed* was created in Montreal, Quebec? Released by Ubisoft Montreal in 2007, the award-winning video game is the brainchild of creative director Patrice Désilets and producer Jade Raymond, both of whom are from Montreal, as well as American writer Corey May. The *Assassin's Creed* franchise now includes over 20 video-game sequels and a movie.

1,000,000

97,856 👍 5,300 💬

First 100 million YouTube views

Avril Lavigne's video for her song "Girlfriend," released in 2007, was the first music video to reach (and surpass) 100 million views on YouTube.

Most popular Canadian gamer

Look no further than Evan Fong, aka, VanossGaming. His 24.9 million YouTube subscribers placed him fourth in the world among gamer accounts in 2020 and *Business Insider* placed him 20th in the world when accounting for all YouTube channels. In 2017 *Forbes* ranked him second in the world in YouTube earnings, at $15.5 million, with some brands paying up to $450,000 to appear in his videos.

▶ YouTube

Most popular Canadian Minecraft player

You may not have heard of Mitchell Donnell-Ralph Hughes, but nearly six million subscribers have heard of this YouTube gamer who goes by the moniker BajanCanadian — a reference to his Barbados-Canadian background. Born in Montreal, Quebec, in 1994, Hughes is Canada's most popular Minecraft player. His channel is full of Minecraft mini-games videos, including his most popular *Hunger Games* parody music video.

Largest known collection of video games

Syd Bolton, from Brantford, Ontario, was the ultimate gamer. Bolton was such a video-game aficionado that over the years he had acquired over 15,000 different titles — the second-largest known collection of video games. In 2005, Bolton opened Canada's very first Personal Computer Museum, dedicated to preserving the history of computers. In addition to Bolton's collection of video games, the museum houses the biggest collection of computers in the country.

Wayne Gretzky

Wayne Gretzky — 'nuff said! But if you need more, the man who many consider to be the greatest hockey player ever holds or shares 61 records in the National Hockey League. Some highlights:

Most points	2,857 (1,487 games, 894 goals, 1,963 assists)
Most points, including playoffs	3,239 (2,856 regular season, 382 playoff)
Most goals	894
Most goals, including playoffs	1,016 (894 regular season, 122 playoff)
Most assists	1,963
Most assists, including playoffs	2,223 (1,963 regular season, 260 playoff)
Most consecutive 40-or-more-goal seasons	12 (1979–80 to 1990–91)
Most consecutive 60-or-more-goal seasons	4 (1981–82 to 1984–85)
Most consecutive 100-or-more-point seasons	13 (1979–80 to 1991–92)

Single-season Records	
Most points, one season	215 (1985–86, 80-game schedule)
Most points, one season, including playoffs	255 (1984–85; 208 points in 80 regular-season games and 47 points in 18 playoff games)
Most goals, one season	92 (1981–82, 80-game schedule)
Most goals, one season, including playoffs	100 (1983–84, 87 goals in 74 regular-season games and 13 goals in 19 playoff games)
Most goals, 50 games from start of season	61 (1981–82 and 1983–84)
Most three-or-more-goal games	10 (1981–82, six three-goal games; three four-goal games; one five-goal game)
Longest consecutive point-scoring streak	51 games — 61 goals, 92 assists for 153 points (October 5, 1983, to January 28, 1984)

Career records: playoffs	
Most playoff goals	122
Most playoff assists	260
Most playoff points	382 (122 goals, 260 assists)
Most game-winning goals in playoffs	24
Most points, one playoff year	47 (1985, 17 goals and 30 assists in 18 games)
Most points in final series	13 (1988, four games plus suspended game vs. Boston, 3 goals and 10 assists)

First indoor hockey game

The first hockey game played on an indoor ice rink between two teams was on March 3, 1875. It took place at Victoria Skating Rink in Montreal. It's thought that the game as we know it was formed in Montreal according to rules developed by James George Aylwin Creighton.

First black hockey player

Willie O'Ree was the first black player in the National Hockey League. His first game was January 18, 1958. O'Ree, born in Fredericton on October 15, 1935, played two seasons for the Boston Bruins (1957–58 and 1960–61) and scored four goals and tallied 10 assists.

First father and son in Hockey Hall of Fame

Bobby Hull and his son Brett became the first father and son inducted into the Hockey Hall of Fame when Brett joined the Hall on November 9, 2009. Brett recorded 1,391 points in 1,269 regular-season games. Bobby tallied 1,170 points in 1,063 regular-season games.

First radio hockey

"He shoots, he scores!" While it's still a matter of debate, the Hockey Hall of Fame reports that the very first radio broadcast of a hockey game took place on February 16, 1923. Legendary announcer Foster Hewitt called the action of the game between Kitchener and Toronto at the Arena Gardens on Toronto station CFCA.

First instant replay

Did you see that? Now you did, thanks to the invention of instant replay by the CBC in 1955. The technique was first used (where else?) on a broadcast of *Hockey Night in Canada*.

Million-dollar hockey player

Bobby Hull was the first hockey player to sign a contract worth over $1 million. He accepted the contract with the Winnipeg Jets, then part of the World Hockey Association, on June 27, 1972, at the corner of Portage and Main in Winnipeg, Manitoba.

First goalie mask

The first person known to wear a goalie mask in a hockey game? Bet you didn't know it was Elizabeth Graham. In 1927, Graham used a fencing mask to protect her face.

First professional goalie mask

The first professional hockey player to wear a goalie mask was Clint Benedict. Benedict, who played for the Montreal Maroons, is believed to have worn a mask for a game or two in the 1929–30 season.

Popularizing the goalie mask

Usually one too many shots to the head does not lead to innovation. But for Canadian Jacques Plante, goaltender for the Montreal Canadiens, getting hit in the face by one more puck on November 1, 1959, was the last straw. After getting stitched up, Plante returned to the game wearing the mask pictured here, and thus began the popularization of the equipment.

Youngest to 100 points

Sidney Crosby of the Pittsburgh Penguins became the youngest NHLer to score 100 points (goals and assists) when he tabbed an assist on a Ryan Malone goal in the Penguins' 6–1 victory over the New York Islanders. It was Pittsburgh's second-last game of the season, and Crosby's record-setting point came when he was 18 years and 253 days old. Crosby added a goal and an assist against Toronto in Pittsburgh's final game of the season to end the campaign with 102 points — one shy of Dale Hawerchuk's record for most NHL points before turning 19.

First to score 500 goals

Maurice "Rocket" Richard, who played his entire career for the Montreal Canadiens, was the first professional hockey player to score 50 goals in 50 games (in 1945–46), but he was also the first professional to score 500 career goals (he tallied his 500th on October 19, 1957). When Richard retired, he'd scored 544 goals.

First state funeral

Maurice Richard holds a very unique distinction for a Canadian athlete. After his death on May 27, 2000, Richard was given a state funeral by his home province of Quebec, which was broadcast live across the country — the first time such an honour was bestowed on a Canadian athlete.

The oldest sports trophy

The Stanley Cup, which is awarded to the champion of the National Hockey League, is the oldest trophy competed for by professional athletes in North America. The trophy was established in 1892 by Sir Frederick Arthur Stanley (Lord Stanley), to be presented to the top hockey club in the Dominion of Canada. NHL teams became the exclusive competitors for the Cup in 1926. The Montreal Canadiens have won the most Cups, claiming 24 between their first win in 1916 and their last, in 1993.

Engraving the Stanley Cup

Engraving the names of the winning team's roster on the Stanley Cup has become a tradition. The custom began in 1907, when the Montreal Wanderers became the first to do so, but it wasn't until 1924 that the ritual was performed annually.

Coach with most Stanley Cups

Legendary hockey coach Scotty Bowman, born in Montreal on September 18, 1933, has won more Stanley Cups than any other coach. His nine championships — five with Montreal (1973, 1976, 1977, 1978, 1979), one with Pittsburgh (1992) and three with Detroit (1997, 1998 and 2002) — also tie him with basketball coach Red Auerbach for the most championships in North America's four major pro sports leagues.

Longest-running TV sports program

Television trivia time. Name the longest-running sports program in television history? It's *Hockey Night in Canada*. The show, on radio since 1933, made its television debut on October 11, 1952, airing a game between the Montreal Canadiens and the Detroit Red Wings.

Most defenseman top scores

Bobby Orr, born in Parry Sound, Ontario, on March 20, 1948, is the only defenceman to lead the National Hockey League in regular-season scoring. Orr accomplished the feat twice, in 1969–70 (120 points) and in 1974–75 (122 points).

Run of eight world championships

Talk about a sports dynasty. The first eight women's world hockey championship tournaments were won by Canada. Canada beat the American team in each championship game, from the inaugural tournament in Ottawa in 1990 to the Halifax/ Dartmouth event in 2004. (The 2003 tournament slated for Beijing, China, was cancelled.)

First woman to play in the NHL

Manon Rhéaume became the first woman to play with an NHL team when the 20-year-old netminder appeared in one period for the Tampa Bay Lightning during a preseason game against the St. Louis Blues in 1992. Seen by some as a shameless publicity sunt, the appearance (another of which was given Rhéaume in the following preseason) is still viewed as one of many important moments in women's hockey.

First woman inducted to Hockey Hall of Fame

Canadian Angela James became one of the first two women inducted into the Hockey Hall of Fame when she and American Cammi Granato were so honoured in 2010. (James and Granato were similarly honoured together in 2008 with induction to the International Ice Hockey Hall of Fame.) James was revered for her remarkable goal scoring, often being called "the Wayne Gretzky of women's hockey."

First all-female broadcast team for NHL game

On International Women's Day in 2020, play-by-play voice Leah Hextall, colour commentator Cassie Campbell-Pascall and reporter Christine Simpson, as well as a 28-member production crew, became the first all-female team to broadcast a major North American sport when they worked the Vegas Golden Knights–Calgary Flames game for Sportsnet. The group were followed shortly after by an all-female American crew who called the Chicago Blackhawks–St. Louis Blues game for NBC.

Back-to-back Olympic-winning goals

Marie-Philip Poulin rocketed to Canadian superstardom after stunning back-to-back performances in Olympic gold-medal games. In 2010, Poulin scored the only goals in Canada's 2–0 gold-medal victory over the rival Americans. At the 2014 Games in Sochi, again against the USA, Poulin dramatically notched the game-tying goal in the final minute of the third period. She then one-upped herself by scoring the gold-medal winner in overtime to give Canada its fourth straight Olympic gold medal in women's ice hockey.

World's best female player

Hayley Wickenheiser, born August 12, 1978, in Shaunavon, Saskatchewan, is Canada's all-time leader in international goals (168), assists (211), and points (379). She competed in the first five Olympic Games in which women's hockey was included, winning gold in all but one tournament (the first, in 1998, where Canada claimed silver), and was named MVP in the 2002 and 2006 Games. In between, Wickenheiser also played for Kirkkonummen Salamat in the second division of the men's Finnish Elite League where she became the first woman to score a goal in men's pro hockey. Wickenheiser was inducted into both the Hockey Hall of Fame and the International Ice Hockey Hall of Fame in 2019.

First gold

Greatest basketball team

In 2015 the Canadian women's basketball team ousted the world No. 1 American squad to capture gold at the Pan American Games. It was the first time Canada has ever won gold on such a big stage. The women's best previous finish was a silver at the 1999 Pan Am Games. The 2015 squad was led by Hamilton, Ontario's, Kia Nurse, whose 33 points paved the way for Canada's historic 81–73 win. Canada's win on home soil marked the first time the home side had won since the U.S. won in Indianapolis in 1987.

James Naismith called the Edmonton Grads "the finest basketball team that ever stepped out on a floor." Between 1915 and 1940, the Edmonton Commercial Graduates, a women's team often referred to as the greatest basketball team ever, played 522 games the world over and won 502, including 147 straight victories. The Grads also won seven of nine games against men's teams.

First NBA game

The first National Basketball Association game was played in Canada. On November 1, 1946, the New York Knickerbockers beat the Toronto Huskies 68–66 at Toronto's Maple Leaf Gardens.

First Canadian NBA champions

The Toronto Raptors snagged their first NBA title in 2019 by besting five-time NBA Championship winners the Golden State Warriors 114–110 in Game 6 of the Finals. But the team's good fortune didn't stop there. The Raptors would enter the 2019–20 season with a record-breaking 15-game winning streak, setting both a franchise and a Canadian professional sports record.

Canadian basketball

When it comes to quintessential Canadian sports, basketball doesn't immediately spring to mind. But the sport was invented by a Canadian, Dr. James Naismith, who was born November 6, 1861, in Almonte, Ontario. He came up with the game in 1891 and it was first played on December 21 of that year at Springfield College in Massachusetts.

First Canadian NBA MVP

Steve Nash was the first Canadian to win the Most Valuable Player award in the National Basketball Association. Nash, a Vancouver native born on February 7, 1974, captured the award in the 2004–05 season, then again the following year. He was only the ninth player in the league's history to win back-to-back MVP awards and only the third guard to win the award multiple times.

First Canadian CY Award

You could call him the ace of Canadian aces. Baseball pitcher Ferguson Jenkins, born in Chatham, Ontario, on December 12, 1942, was the first Canadian to win the Cy Young Award, awarded annually to the game's best pitcher. Jenkins nabbed the honour while pitching for the Chicago Cubs in 1971. Éric Gagné, in 2003, is the only other Canadian to win the award.

First Canadian in Baseball Hall of Fame

Pitcher Ferguson Jenkins was the first Canadian elected to the American National Baseball Hall of Fame in Cooperstown, New York, in 1987. Jenkins won 284 games — including a stretch of 20 a year for six straight seasons — and was the first pitcher in history to strike out more than 3,000 batters and walk less than 1,000 batters.

Babe Ruth's first pro homer

Legendary baseball player Babe Ruth hit his first professional home run in Toronto. On September 5, 1914, as a 19-year-old rookie in the International League, Ruth hit that monumental homer at Maple Leaf Park on the Toronto Islands.

Canadian MLB MVPs

Three Canadians have won a Major League Baseball MVP award. The first was Larry Walker of Maple Ridge, British Columbia, who won the NL MVP in 1997. The next was Justin Morneau of New Westminster, British Columbia, who won the AL MVP in 2006. He was followed by Toronto's Joey Votto, seen here, who was voted as the 2010 NL MVP.

First Canadian World Series win

In 1992, the Toronto Blue Jays became the first non-American team to win baseball's World Series championship. They defeated the Atlanta Braves on October 24 to claim the title. The team repeated the feat in 1993. Pictured here is outfielder Joe Carter.

First black ballplayer in MLB

Jackie Robinson, the first black baseball player in Major League Baseball in the modern era, played his first professional games for the Montreal Royals in 1946. A minor-league affiliate of the Brooklyn Dodgers — the team Robinson would debut with in the majors — the Royals won the International League title that season.

First Canadian team in Major League Baseball

The Montreal Expos (seen here in 1988) were the first Canadian team to join Major League Baseball, in 1969. In 2004, the team was relocated to Washington, D.C., and renamed the Washington Nationals.

279

First triple Lutz

Don Jackson of Oshawa, Ontario, was the first person to land a triple Lutz jump in competition. He performed the feat on March 15, 1962, at the World Figure Skating Championship in Prague, Czech Republic. It was another 12 years before the jump was repeated in competition.

First perfect seven

That first triple Lutz performed by Don Jackson wasn't his only amazing "first." At the end of his performance at the 1962 championship where he unveiled the triple Lutz, Jackson received seven perfect scores (6.0) from the judges, the highest tally ever.

First world figure skating champion

Don Jackson wasn't done there. His perfect score won him the 1962 World Figure Skating Championship, and made him the first Canadian man to do so.

First death spiral

Canadian figure skating duo Suzanne Morrow and Wallace Distelmeyer were the first team to execute the modern-day death spiral in an international competition. They performed the move at the 1948 World Figure Skating Championships in Davos, Switzerland.

First quadruple jump

He put a whole new spin on things. In 1988, at the World Figure Skating Championship in Budapest, Hungary, Kurt Browning, born in Rocky Mountain House, Alberta, on June 18, 1966, performed the first quadruple jump in competition in the sport's history. Oh, he won the championship, too.

First cereal box appearance

Kurt Browning was the first Canadian athlete to appear on the front of an American cereal box. He graced the front of Special K in 1998.

First double Lutz

Figure skater Barbara Ann Scott, born in Ottawa in 1928, was the first woman to land a double Lutz jump in competition, which she did in 1942. The jump later helped her capture the gold medal at the 1948 Winter Olympics in St. Moritz, Switzerland. Scott was also the first non-European to win a world championship in skating in 1947.

Most Olympic medals

Tessa Virtue and Scott Moir are the winningest figure skaters in Olympic history. Their five medals (three gold and two silver) are more than any other figure skater has won. The beloved pair sealed the deal with two gold medals (dance and team) at the 2018 Games in South Korea.

First Olympic gold for hockey

The Winnipeg Falcons were the first team to win an Olympic gold medal in hockey, in 1920 in Antwerp, Belgium. At the time, the winner of the Allan Cup, awarded to the nation's top senior men's amateur hockey club, was selected to represent the country at the Games. The Falcons dominated the tournament, besting Czechoslovakia 15–0, the United States 2–0 and Sweden 12–1 to claim gold. At the time the event was held in the summer.

First Olympic gold

George W. Orton of Strathroy, Ontario, won the nation's first Olympic gold medal at the Paris Games in 1900, despite the fact that Canada did not send a team to the event. Orton was asked to join the American team, thanks to his many victories at track and field meets throughout the United States, and he reached the top of the podium in the 2,500 m steeplechase. He also won bronze in the 400 m hurdles at the Games.

First three-medal sprinter

Andre De Grasse became the first Canadian sprinter to earn three medals in one Olympic Games when he captured two bronze and one silver at the 2016 Rio Games. His outstanding running placed him ahead of Canadian legends Donovan Bailey (two medals in 1996) and Percy Williams (two medals in 1928).

First gold medal on home soil

On February 14, 2010, Alexandre Bilodeau became the first Canadian athlete to capture a gold medal on home soil when he placed first in the men's moguls event at Cypress Mountain at the 2010 Vancouver Olympics. Bilodeau's performance was the first of 14 such gold-medal performances for Canada in Vancouver, which set a new record for gold medal winners in a single Winter Games. Norway and Germany have since tied Canada, with 14 golds apiece at PyeongChang, South Korea, in 2018.

First Olympic team

The 1904 Olympic Games in St. Louis marked the first time Canada sent an official team to the event. The 43-member team won six medals: four gold, a silver and a bronze. The gold medals came in soccer, lacrosse, 56-pound weight throw and golf.

First female Olympic shooter

Born in Medicine Hat, Alberta, on November 5, 1950, Susan Nattrass was the first woman to ever compete in the Olympics in a shooting event (shooting was open to both sexes until 1992). She placed 25th in the trap event at the 1976 Games in Montreal.

First Canadian sub-10-second Olympic sprinter

That should say first *legal* sub-10-second Olympic sprinter, because Ben Johnson is not who we are here to talk about. It was Donovan Bailey who ran the 100 m race at the 1996 Atlanta Olympics in a blistering 9.84 seconds, setting a new world record in the process. Needless to say, he took the gold in the event, and he and the Canadian relay team did the same in the 4x100 m event.

Most medals at one Olympics

Cindy Klassen holds the Canadian record for winning the most medals (five) at one Olympic Games. She reached the podium in the following long-track speed skating events in Turin, Italy, in 2006: 1,000 m, 1,500 m, 3,000 m, 5,000 m and team pursuit. Her haul is also the most ever won by a female speed skater (Ireen Wüst of the Netherlands tied Klassen with five medals of her own at the 2014 Sochi Games).

First alpine gold

Anne Heggtveit, born in Ottawa on January 11, 1939, won Canada's first-ever gold medal in alpine skiing, which was also the first North American gold in slalom. She captured the medal at the 1960 Olympic Games in Squaw Valley, California.

Multiple medals

Clara Hughes (see right) and fellow speed skater Cindy Klassen are tied as the most-decorated Canadian Olympians. Each won six medals: Hughes captured four bronze (two in speed skating, two in cycling), one silver and one gold (both speed skating); Klassen nabbed three bronze, two silver and one gold, all in speed skating.

Soccer stars

Led by the tough as nails Christine Sinclair, the Canadian women's soccer team captured back-to-back Olympic bronze medals at the 2008 and 2012 Games. They were Canada's first medals in soccer since the Canadian men's side captured gold in 1904!

First individual Winter Olympic gold for men

Speed skater Gaétan Boucher, born in Charlesbourg, Quebec, on May 10, 1958, was the first Canadian man to win an individual gold medal at the Winter Olympic Games. In fact, he won two gold medals (one in 1,000 m and one in 1,500 m) at the 1984 Games in Sarajevo, Bosnia and Herzegovina.

Medals in winter and summer

There are few athletes that reach the pinnacle of multiple sports. Canadian Olympic athlete Clara Hughes, however, is one of the world's finest exceptions. Hughes is the only Olympian ever to win multiple medals at both the Summer and Winter Games. In speed skating she captured four medals (one gold, one silver and two bronze) in three Olympics (2002, 2006 and 2010). As a cyclist, Hughes won bronze in both the road race and time trial events in Atlanta in 1996.

Crazy Canuck winner

As a member of the Crazy Canucks (the nickname for Canada's team of top competitive skiers of the 1970s and 1980s), Steve Podborski of Toronto was the first male non-European skier to win the World Cup downhill championship, which he accomplished in 1982. Over his career, Podborski captured eight World Cup race wins and a bronze medal in downhill at the Lake Placid Olympics in 1980.

First world skiing champ

Skier Lucile Wheeler, born on January 14, 1935, in St-Jovite, Quebec, was the first North American to win a World Ski Championship. She captured first in both downhill and giant slalom at the events in Bad Gastein, Austria, in February 1958. She was also the first Canadian to win a medal in downhill at the Olympics — bronze in 1956 at Cortina d'Ampezzo, Italy.

First to win gold in Summer and Winter Paralympics

Viviane Forest snagged her first gold medal in 2000 as a member of the Canadian gold-ball team (goldball is a game for visually impaired athletes wherein teams try to score on each other with a sound-emitting ball). Forest then turned heads in Vancouver in 2010 when she nabbed five medals (one gold, three silver and one bronze) in her Paralympic debut in para alpine skiing. She's pictured here with her guide, Lindsay Debou.

First to win gold in two ⋯⋯⋯ different summer sports

Athlete-turned-politician Michelle Stilwell was the first Paralympian to win gold in two separate sports. Her first came in 2000 at the Sydney Games when she and her teammates claimed the top prize in wheelchair basketball. Her second came in Beijing in 2008 when she won gold in both the 100 m and 200 m wheelchair races. For good measure, she collected more gold in both London (2012) and Rio (2016).

Most medals (female)

Today she is a Canadian parliamentarian, but Chantal Petitclerc is better known to many as the most decorated female Paralympian this country has ever produced. In five Games from 1992 to 2008, her 21 medals (14 gold, five silver, and two bronze) tie her with Michael Edgson as the most decorated Paralympian. Petitclerc was named Canada's best athlete in 2008, becoming the third athlete with a disability, after Terry Fox and Rick Hansen, to receive the honour.

Most medals (male)

Michael Edgson snagged 21 Paralympic medals (18 gold and three silver) across the 1984, 1988 and 1992 Games, with a Canadian-record haul of nine golds in the 1988 Seoul Paralympics. In 2015 he was enshrined in Canada's Sports Hall of Fame.

Most winter medals in one Paralympics

Mark Arendz of Hartsville, Prince Edward Island, won six medals across biathlon and cross-country — one gold, two silver, and three bronze — at PyeongChang in 2018 to become the Canadian with the most medals in a single Winter Paralympic Games. He was honoured with carrying the Canadian flag at the closing ceremonies.

Top winter performer

At the PyeongChang Games on March 12, 2018, Brian McKeever became Canada's top winter Paralympian by claiming gold in the 20 km free visually impaired cross-country ski race. The medal was his 17th overall (13 of which are gold). Legally blind since 2001, McKeever has participated in every Winter Paralympics since Salt Lake in 2002. In 2018 he was Canada's flag bearer for the opening ceremony. McKeever is pictured here with his guide, Graham Nishikawa.

▶▶ *Sports*

First Canadian Grand Prix win

Race car driver Gilles Villeneuve, born on January 18, 1950, in Chambly, Quebec, was the first Canadian to win a Grand Prix event. Villeneuve won the Formula One race in Montreal, the Canadian Grand Prix, on October 8, 1978. The track is now named after him. Villeneuve died in a crash during a qualifying session for the Belgian Grand Prix on May 8, 1982. Gilles' son Jacques grabbed headlines in 1997 when he became the first Canadian to win the season-long Formula One championship in 1997.

First Canadian Grand Prix

Formula One cars first raced in Canada at the inaugural Canadian Grand Prix on August 27, 1967, at the Mosport race track — today called the Canadian Tire Motorsport Park — in Bowmanville, Ontario. Jack Brabham of Australia won that first race.

First sports association

The National Lacrosse Association was Canada's first sports association. It was established on September 26, 1867, in Kingston, Ontario.

First yacht club

The Royal Halifax Yacht Club was the first yacht club in North America. Its beginnings date back to July 1837, though it wasn't officially established as the RHYC until 1861. In 1922, the club became the Royal Nova Scotia Yacht Squadron.

First sporting club

The first sporting club in Canada was the Royal Montreal Curling Club, which was founded in 1807.

First five-pin bowling

The invention of five-pin bowling, a Canadian concept, was the result of dissatisfaction with the American 10-pin version of the game. Thomas F. (Tommy) Ryan opened the first regulation 10-pin lanes in Toronto in 1905, but customers complained about the size and weight of the balls. Ryan began experimenting with different pin and ball sizes, and, in 1909, Canada's superior five-pin game was born.

Oldest football team

The NFL may predate the CFL by almost 40 years, but that doesn't mean football wasn't being played in Canada. In fact, Canada is home to the world's oldest continually operating football team, the Toronto Argonauts. The team was formed in 1873 by members of the Argonaut Rowing Club who wanted to play rugby. The sport and team evolved over the years and even predates the oldest continually operating American football team, the Arizona Cardinals, who were founded in the Chicago area in 1898.

▶▶ *Sports*

First synchronized ········ swimming

Ornamental swimming, anyone? Montreal hosted the first synchronized swimming competition ever — called ornamental or figure swimming at the time — in 1924. The event was a provincial championship, which was won by Peg Seller, who was also a top Canadian diver and water polo player.

Double whammy

Hank Biasatti is the only Canadian to play at the major-league level in both basketball and baseball. Aside from playing with basketball's Toronto Huskies in 1946, Biasatti played professional baseball for the Philadelphia Athletics in 1949.

···· Toughest boxer

None other than Muhammad Ali, considered the greatest heavyweight boxer ever, called Canadian boxer George Chuvalo "the toughest man I ever fought." Chuvalo, born on September 12, 1937, in Toronto, was the sport's Canadian heavyweight champion from September 1958 until he retired in 1979. While he never captured the world title, in 97 professional matches, Chuvalo was never knocked out or down — even in two losses to Ali.

World heavyweight boxing champion

He's Canada's only world heavyweight boxing champion. Tommy Burns, born in Hanover, Ontario, on June 17, 1881, won the world title on February 23, 1906, in a 20-round decision over Marvin Hart in Los Angeles. He held the championship until December 26, 1908, when he was defeated by Jack Johnson — the first black fighter to hold the world heavyweight title — in 14 rounds in Sydney, Australia.

Canada's first fastest man

He was Canada's first recorded fastest man: Harry Winston Jerome, born on September 30, 1940, in Prince Albert, Saskatchewan, was the first Canadian to officially hold a world track record. In 1960, at just 19, Jerome ran the 100 m in 10 seconds at the Canadian Olympic Trials to tie the world mark. Jerome held several sprinting world records throughout his career.

Jockey wins 500+

Jockey Sandy Hawley, born in Oshawa, Ontario, on April 16, 1949, was the first to win 500 races in one year. Hawley eclipsed the record in 1973, totalling 515 first-place finishes. During his career, Hawley won 6,449 races.

First triple crown

In 1919, Canadian-owned racehorse Sir Barton was the first to win the American Triple Crown — capturing first in each of the Kentucky Derby, Preakness and Belmont Stakes races — although the title didn't exist at the time.

First Canadian to win Derby

Racehorse Northern Dancer, born in Oshawa, Ontario, on May 27, 1961, was the first Canadian-bred horse to win the Kentucky Derby, in 1964. Northern Dancer also won the Preakness Stakes in the same year.

Sports

Tennis champ extraordinaire (doubles)

He's a tennis virtuoso. Daniel Nestor, born on September 4, 1972, is the only player in the game's history to win all four Grand Slams, all of the Masters Series events, the year-end Masters Cup and an Olympic gold medal in doubles.

First Canadian U.S. Open winner (singles)

Nineteen-year-old Bianca Andreescu shook the world on September 7, 2019, when she defeated tennis legend Serena Williams to win her first U.S. Open women's tennis championship, making the Mississauga native Canada's first-ever Grand Slam champion in a singles category.

Canada's best golfer

Look no further than phenom Brooke Henderson, who at 22 has nine LPGA Tour wins, the most by any Canadian man or woman on the PGA or LPGA Tours. She was the Canadian female athlete of the year in 2015, 2017 and 2018, and was the first woman in 45 years to capture the national championship when she did so in 2018. She also snagged her first major at the age of 18, making her the second-youngest woman to win a major.

First transatlantic club

The Toronto Wolfpack of the professional Rugby League, primarily based in the United Kingdom and France, became the first transatlantic professional sports club in the world. The club plays its home games in Toronto at Lamport stadium and plays its away games in Europe. In 2019 the Wolfpack won promotion to the Super League division of Rugby League, the highest division there is.

World champion judoka

Christa Deguchi made Canadian history in 2019 by becoming the nation's first-ever judo world champion. (She also made history in 2018 when she captured the nation's first-ever judo world champion-ship medal — a bronze.) Deguchi won the -57 kg title by defeating the world No. 1 from Japan, Tsukasa Yoshida.

X Games champ

Mark McMorris of Regina, Saskatchewan, tied the all-time record for individual X Games medals with his 18th — a silver in the big air competition at the 2020 Games. Before capturing the silver, McMorris had earned eight gold (five in slopestyle, three in big air), six silver (three in big air, three in slopestyle) and three bronze medals (two in slopestyle, one in big air). His 18th medal ties him with American Shaun White.

Festivals

Top docs fest

The Hot Docs Canadian International Documentary Festival is North America's largest of its kind. Each year during its late April/early May run, Hot Docs presents more than 180 Canadian and international documentary films. The festival was founded in 1993.

Largest Caribbean festival

If you want to celebrate Caribbean culture in Canada, there's nowhere else to be than Toronto in mid-July and early August. The Toronto Caribbean Carnival, formerly Caribana (and still referred to commonly by that moniker), is considered the largest cultural festival of its kind in North America. The highlight of the three-week festival is Parade Day, where Caribbean-inspired acts from around the world celebrate calypso, soca, reggae, hip hop, chutney, steel and brass bands.

Most pride

Toronto has held a Pride parade every year since 1981, with average attendance swelling to more than one million in 2019. In 2014, the city became the first in North America to host the World Pride Festival, an international celebration of lesbian, gay, bisexual, transsexual, transgender, queer, asexual and two-spirit individuals.

Top film fest

The Toronto International Film Festival, held annually in September, is considered one of the most important film festivals in the world. It's certainly the premier festival in North America. Launched in 1976, internationally, it ranks second, after France's Cannes Film Festival.

First film festival

Saskatchewan's Yorkton Film Festival, established as the Yorkton International Film Festival in 1947, was the first film festival in North America. The festival, held each May, was created by James Lysyshyn, a field officer for the National Film Board, and it's still going strong today.

Canada's largest winter carnival

The Quebec Winter Carnival is the second-largest winter carnival in the world. Held annually from late January through mid-February, the first festival took place in 1894, but the present-day incarnation of the event was established in 1955. The carnival features a variety of winter sports, snow sculptures and activities based on Quebec traditions.

Biggest jazz festival

The Montreal International Jazz Festival is considered the largest in the world. Held annually in late June/early July since 1982, the modern festival hosts 3,000 musicians from 30 countries, holds more than 1,000 concerts and attracts nearly two million visitors.

▶▶ *Festivals*

Largest fringe festival

The Edmonton International Fringe Theatre Festival was the first such festival and it is the largest in North America and the second largest in the world. It's been held each August since 1982.

Most country music

It's possible they're biased, but Alberta Travel claims the Big Valley Jamboree is the largest outdoor music festival in North America. Held annually in midsummer since 1993 in Camrose, southeast of Edmonton, the four-day country music fest has hosted a who's who of the genre's top acts.

Largest tattoo show

This isn't a show about *getting* tattooed. No, the Royal Nova Scotia International Tattoo is inspired by military band shows. Billed as the world's largest annual indoor show, the Tattoo is held during the first week of July and features a variety of entertainment, including bagpipes, highland dancers, military displays, acrobats and more. The Tattoo has been held yearly since 1979.

Most Elvis

Elvis lives! At least he does at the Collingwood Elvis Festival, held each July in Ontario since 1995. It's the world's largest festival celebrating legendary singer Elvis Presley. The highlight of the event is the Elvis impersonator contest, which attracts many of the world's best Elvis tribute artists.

Top community event

The Canadian National Exhibition (CNE), held each year in Toronto since 1879, is the nation's largest annual community event. The CNE is one of the top five agricultural fairs on the continent. It attracts more than 1.5 million visitors annually.

Photo fest

The annual CONTACT Photography Festival is the largest photography event in the world. Held each May in the Greater Toronto Area, it showcases the works of more than 1,500 Canadian and international shutterbugs through over 200 exhibitions and programming. The festival, which has an estimated audience of 1.8 million, was founded in 1997.

Festivals

Most blooms

Get your garden on. Canada Blooms is the largest flower and garden festival in Canada. Held annually in March since 1997, the exhibition now attracts more than 200,000 visitors. Among many exhibits are fantasy gardens created by the world's top designers.

Largest maple syrup celebration

Recognized by Guinness World Records in 2000, when 66,529 people attended the event, the Elmira Maple Syrup Festival is the largest of its kind. First held in 1965, the annual event attracts thousands each year to eat pancakes and sample maple syrup.

First agricultural fair

The first agricultural fair in North America was held in Windsor, Nova Scotia, in May 1765. The Hants County Exhibition still takes place each September, making it the oldest continuously run agricultural exhibition on the continent.

Longest rink and then some

At 7.8 km long, the frozen Rideau Canal makes the longest ice rink in the world, and to skate it is a focal point of Winterlude. The winter festival, held annually in Ottawa and Gatineau, Quebec, also features ice sculpture and the ever-popular Snowflake Kingdom. Constructed each year in Jacques Cartier Park, the kingdom includes gigantic snow slides, a winter obstacle course, a giant maze and much more.

Largest agricultural fair

The Royal Agricultural Winter Fair, held annually in November in Toronto, is the largest combined indoor agricultural fair and international equestrian competition in the world. The first Royal opened on November 22, 1922, with 17,000 entries and drew more than 150,000 visitors. Today the fair takes up nearly 93,000 m^2 of space and attract thousands of entries and about 300,000 visitors.

World's largest axe
Nackawic, New Brunswick

World's largest beaver
Beaverlodge, Alberta

World's largest badminton racket
St. Albert, Alberta

World's largest bee
Falher, Alberta

World's largest blueberry
Oxford, Nova Scotia

World's largest bunnock
Macklin, Saskatchewan

World's largest burl
Port McNeill, British Columbia

World's largest chainsaw
Lillooet, British Columbia

World's largest Adirondack chair
Varney, Ontario

World's largest Muskoka chair
Gravenhurst, Ontario

World's largest chuckwagon
Dewberry, Alberta

World's largest claim post
Cobalt, Ontario

World's largest cookie jar
Deloraine, Manitoba

World's largest cross-country skis
100 Mile House, British Columbia

World's largest curling rock
Arborg, Manitoba

World's largest Coke can
Portage la Prairie, Manitoba

World's largest conch
Caraquet, New Brunswick

World's largest cuckoo clock
Kimberley, British Columbia

World's largest dinosaur
Drumheller, Alberta

▶▶ Roadside Attractions

World's largest dragonfly
Wabamun, Alberta

World's largest endangered ferruginous hawk
Leader, Saskatchewan

World's largest fiddle
Sydney, Nova Scotia

World's largest fiddleheads
Plaster Rock, New Brunswick

World's largest fire hydrant
Elm Creek, Manitoba

World's largest fly rod
Houston, British Columbia

World's largest gold pan
Quesnel, British Columbia

World's largest golf bag
Orangeville, Ontario

World's largest golf tee
Trochu, Alberta

Canada's largest goose
Wawa, Ontario

World's largest hockey cards
Kelvington, Saskatchewan

World's largest hockey stick and puck
Duncan, British Columbia

World's largest honeybee
Tisdale, Saskatchewan

World's largest inukshuk
Schomberg, Ontario

World's largest lamp
Donalda, Alberta

World's largest lobster
Shediac, New Brunswick

World's largest mallard
Andrew, Alberta

World's largest maple leaf
Millville, New Brunswick

World's largest mastodon
Stewiacke, Nova Scotia

World's largest moose
Moose Jaw, Saskatchewan

World's largest wooden nickel
Boiestown, New Brunswick

World's largest oil can
Rocanville, Saskatchewan

World's largest orchard ladder
Summerland, British Columbia

World's largest painting on easel
Altona, Manitoba

World's largest paper clip
Kipling, Saskatchewan

World's largest perogy
Glendon, Alberta

World's second-largest smoking pipe
Saint Claude, Manitoba

World's largest purple martin colony
Neepawa, Manitoba

World's largest putter
Bow Island, Alberta

▶▶ *Roadside Attractions*

The wall (world's largest photo mosaic)
Port Carling, Ontario

World's largest railroad spike
Hines Creek, Alberta

World's largest rooster
Shediac, New Brunswick

Worlds largest Rolls-Royce
Steinbach, Manitoba

World's largest silver fox
Salisbury, New Brunswick

World's largest snowman
Beardmore, Ontario

World's largest softball
Chauvin, Alberta

Canada's largest squid
Glovers Harbour, Newfoundland

World's largest starship *Enterprise*
Vulcan, Alberta

World's largest sturgeon
Dominion City, Manitoba

World's largest sundial
Lloydminster, Saskatchewan

World's tallest teepee
Medicine Hat, Alberta

World's largest tin soldier
New Westminster, British Columbia

World's largest tomahawk
Cut Knife, Saskatchewan

World's largest toonie
Campbellford, Ontario

World's largest totem pole
Alert Bay, British Columbia

World's largest totem pole from a single tree
Victoria, British Columbia

▶▶ Roadside Attractions

World's largest Ukrainian easter egg
Vegreville, Alberta

World's largest totem pole in diameter
Duncan, British Columbia

World's largest wagon wheel and pick
Fort Assiniboine, Alberta

World's largest tree crusher
Mackenzie, British Columbia

World's largest tractor weather vane
Westlock, Alberta

World's largest turtle
Turtleford, Saskatchewan

World's largest western boot
Edmonton, Alberta

Biggest Fun

One-of-a-kind thrill ride

Looking for a unique thrill? The Sledge Hammer ride at Canada's Wonderland is one of a kind. The attraction, sometimes called a "giant jumping machine," lifts riders 24.3 m in the air in eight-person gondolas that take them through a series of jumps and free falls lasting 1 minute and 43 seconds, reaching a top speed of 65 km per hour.

WindSeeker swing ride

Canada's Wonderland's WindSeeker swing ride, which ascends 91.7 m and swings riders at a 45-degree angle at speeds of up to 50 km per hour, was the first such ride in the world. The ride lasts three minutes.

Leviathan

Look no further than Canada's Wonderland for the longest, tallest and fastest roller coaster in the nation. Leviathan, which debuted in 2012, is 1,672 m long, 93.3 m tall, and can hit a top speed of 148 km per hour!

Yukon Striker

In 2019, Canada's Wonderland opened the world's longest, tallest and fastest dive coaster. The Yukon Striker is 1,105 m long and dives 75 m into an underwater tunnel! As if that weren't enough, this thrill ride tops out at 130 km per hour!

Biggest indoor triple-loop roller coaster

West Edmonton Mall boasts the world's largest indoor triple-loop roller coaster, the Mindbender, which is part of the mall's Galaxyland amusement park.

Largest indoor lake

As you already know, West Edmonton Mall has a lot of big achievements, one of which is that it is also home to the world's largest permanent indoor lake. The lake includes an exact replica of the *Santa Maria*, the flagship of Christopher Columbus' 1492 expedition to North America.

Largest indoor waterpark

West Edmonton Mall is also home to World Waterpark, the largest of its kind in North America (and second largest in the world) at nearly 21,000 m²!

Largest outdoor wave pool

White Water Bay at the Splash Works water park in Canada's Wonderland is the largest outdoor wave pool in the nation. It would take 90 gallons of paint to paint the bottom of the pool.

Largest indoor ···· miniature golf course

West Edmonton Mall is home to the world's largest indoor miniature golf course. Professor Wem's Adventure Golf Course features 18 holes, complete with sand traps and water hazards.

PHOTO CREDITS

t = top; m = middle; b = bottom; l = left; c = centre; r = right; bi = background image

Shutterstock

front cover: furtseff; **back cover:** tai11; pp. 8–9 bi: dreamcatcher; p. 9 tl: Marcel Comeau; p. 9 mr: Steve Norman; p. 10 t: Marius M. Grecu; p. 10 b: Sergey STC; p. 11 b: SF photo; p. 12 tl: Mr.Somchai Sukkasem; p. 12 tr: A. Michael Brown; p. 12 b: Constantine Androsoff; p. 13: Timothy Yue; p. 14 t: gvictoria; p. 14 b: Akshay-PhotOvation; p. 15 t: Melinda Fawver; p. 15 bl: Jostein Hauge; p. 15 br: domnitsky; p. 16 t: Serjio74; p. 17 t: mikecphoto; p. 17 m: SF photo; p. 18 t: SF photo; p. 20 b: meunierd; p. 21 t: Sanavi; p. 21 m: JHVE-Photo; p. 21 b: meunierd; p. 22 t: ozmen; p. 22 m: achinthamb; p. 22 b: Paul McKinnon; p. 23 t: Adwo; p. 23 bl: Martchan; p. 23 br: EQRoy; p. 24 t: Piotr Krzeslak; p. 24 b: Ian Maton; p. 25: Pi-Lens; p. 26 t: Kim D. Lyman; p. 27 t: Songquan Deng; p. 27 bl: PPVector; p. 27 bc: ASAG Studio; p. 27 br: Line - design; p. 28: Elena Elisseeva; p. 29 t: Meg Wallace Photography; p. 29 bl: Capricornis Photographic Inc.; p. 29 br: Vintagepix; pp. 30–31 bi: Sebastian Arciszewski; p. 31 t: Josef Hanus; p. 32 tr: Matthew Jacques; p. 32 ml: ggw; p. 33 t: Denis Roger; p. 33 bl: Jeff Whyte; p. 33 br: Nikola Bilic; p. 34 br: Hortimages; p. 35 tl: Robert L. Kothenbeutel; p. 35 b: Dennis W Donohue; p. 36 ml: Wehart; p. 36 bl & br: VoodooDot; pp. 36–37 bi: sutadimages; pp. 38–39 bi: bestber; p. 38 tl: tai11; p. 38 mr: Ritu Manoj Jethani; p. 38 b: Yanas; p. 39 tr: Debby Wong; p. 41 b: Art Babych; p. 42 b: Daniel Prudek; p. 45 tr: Carolina K. Smith MD; p. 46 tl: Anton Starikov; p. 46 tr: New Africa; p. 46 br: OlgaBombologna; p. 47 tl: Chad Hutchinson; p. 47 tr: LunaseeStudios; p. 48 ml: Billion Photos; p. 49 bl: Max Lindenthaler; p. 49 br: Marbury; p. 50 tr: Marijus Auruskevicius; p. 50 ml: CapturePB; p. 50 b: Michael C. Gray; pp. 50–51 bi: 4Max; p. 51 br: restyler; p. 52 tl: irina02; p. 52 ml: Seh Kin Wai; p. 52 bl: Volodymyr Krasyuk; p. 52 br: Maen CG; p. 53 tl: Krasula; p. 53 mr: chrisdorney; p. 54 bl: iyd39; pp. 56–57 bi: Jurik Peter; pp. 58–59 bi: bbernard; p. 59 tr: Chinnapong; pp. 60–61 bi: il67; p. 61: adriaticfoto; p. 62 bl: xiaorui; pp. 62–63 bi: BAIVECTOR; p. 63 t: khuruzero; p. 63 br: keki; p. 65: Tatevosian Yana; pp. 66–67 bi: Norman Pogson; p. 67 bl: ziviani; p. 67 br: fotografermen; pp. 68–69 bi: BAIVECTOR; p. 69 b: thodonal88; p. 70 tl: Kyrylo Glivin; p. 70 br: Canetti; pp. 70–71bi: Mike Rogal; pp. 72–73 bi: Cenz07; p. 74 b: David J. Mitchell; pp. 76–77: Gluiki; pp. 78–79 bi: mexrix; pp. 78–79 frames: Iakov Filimonov; p. 80 b: David Acosta Allely; pp. 80–81 bi: Theus; pp. 84–85 bi: LaiQuocAnh; p. 96 r: Eric Buermeyer; p. 97 l: Nataliia Reshetnikova; p. 99 t: Tudoran Andrei; p. 99 b: Russ Heinl; p. 100 l: Happy Stock Photo; p. 101 m: klarka0608; pp. 102–103 frames: YummyBuum; pp. 106–107 bi: YummyBuum; pp. 106–107 pins: Kovalov Anatolii; pp. 108–109 bi: Apostrophe; pp. 108–109 tape & clips: Kovalov Anatolii; p. 109 b: Art Babych; p. 110: Max Lindenthaler; p. 111 t: Bob Hilscher; p. 111 m: Christian Delbert; p. 111 b: EB Adventure Photography; p. 112 t: Stories In Light; p. 112 b: Tory Kallman; p. 113 t: JPL Designs; p. 113 m: Muskoka Stock Photos; p. 113 b: Josef Hanus; pp. 114–115 bi: Roberto Caucino; p. 115 b: Andrea C. Miller; pp. 116–117 bi: Jing Zhong; p. 117 m: Josef Hanus; p. 118 b: Jeff Whyte; pp. 118–119 bi: Darko-HD Photography; p. 119 b: mmckinneyphotography; p. 120: JOZEF_KAROLY; p. 121 t: Holly Nicoll; p. 121 b: 2009fotofriends; p. 122 m: Bruce Raynor; p. 122 b: Jeff Whyte; pp. 122–123 bi: nienora; p 123 t: alan dyer; p. 123 m: Jeff Whyte; p. 123 b: Protasov AN; p. 124 b: Zoran Karapancev; p. 125 t: Alex JW Robinson; p. 125 b: Blaze986; p. 126: Sonia Dubois; p. 127 t: Swapan Photography; p. 127 ml: innakreativ; p. 127 mr: Kletr; p. 128 l: SBshot87; pp. 128–129 bi: Scott Prokop; p. 129 m: Blaze986; p. 130 b: Cheryl McMullan; p. 131 t: sirtravelalot; p. 131 b: Pictureguy; p. 132 t: Geo-grafika; p. 132 b: siraphat; pp. 132–133 bi: Henryk Sadura; pp. 134–135 bi: SBshot87; p. 136: James William Smith; p. 137 tl: Lana B; p. 137 tr: JL IMAGES; p. 137 bl: JHVEPhoto; p. 137 br: alexskopje; p. 138 tl: Songquan Deng; p. 138 tr: JayTee88; p. 138 b: JHVEPhoto; pp. 138–139 bi: javarman; p. 139 t: Click Images; p. 140 t: Lester Balajadia; p. 140 m: Kiev.Victor; p. 140 b: Petur Asgeirsson; p. 141 t: JohnnyJBoy; p. 141 m: A_Dozmorov; p. 141 b: Lester Balajadia; p. 142: Randi Scott; p. 143 tl: matka_Wariatka; p. 143 tr: Vector things; p. 143 m: JHVEPhoto; p. 143 b: sherwood; p. 144 t: ValeStock; p. 144 m: Spiroview Inc; p. 144 b: Everett Collection; p. 145: dreamcatcher; p. 146: Kathy Hutchins; p. 147 b: IVY PHOTOS; p. 148: Ronnie Chua; p. 149 t: Benoit Daoust; p. 149 b: Pascal Guay; p. 150 t: 279photo Studio; p. 151 t: MaraZe; p. 151 m: Norman Pogson; p. 152 t: BoJack; p. 152 b: EA Photography; p. 153 t: radioshoot, p. 153 b: Veronica Louro; p. 154 bi: Horst Petzold; p. 154 b: Everett Collection; p. 156 t: Bob Hilscher; p. 156 b: Tom Clausen; p. 157 t: Nagel Photography; p. 157 b: vagabond54; pp.

158–159 bi: Tom Clausen; p. 159 m: valleyboi63; p. 159 b: valleyboi63; pp. 160–161 bi: Chiyacat; p. 162 b: vagabond54; pp. 162–163 bi: Albert Pego; p. 163 m: Reimar; p. 163 b: Terry W Ryder; p. 164 tl: EQRoy; p. 164 tr: pancha.me; p. 164 b: Darlene Munro; p. 165: Warren Price Photography; p. 166: leo w kowal; p. 167 t: JHVEPhoto; p. 167 b: MollieGPhoto; p. 168 b: Howard Sandler; pp. 168–169 bi: Darryl Brooks; p. 169 tl: vesilvio; p. 169 tr: TotemArt; p. 169 b: tryton2011; p. 170: Verena Joy; p. 171 t: aapsky; p. 171 b: Jennifer E Geoghan; p. 172: Andrea Leone; p. 173 t: smcfeeters; p. 173 b: Vadim.Petrov; p. 174 b: Paul McKinnon; pp. 174–175 bi: Paul Reeves Photography; pp. 176–177 bi: Volodymyr Kyrylyuk; p. 176 b: rustycanuck; p. 177 t: Olivier Le Queinec; p. 177 ml: SYMPL IMAGES; p. 177 mr: Verena Joy; p. 178 tl: Georgios Kollidas; p.178 tr: kevin brine; p. 178 b: Julie Marshall; p. 179 b: LunaseeStudios; p. 180: Josef Hanus; p. 181: Jiri Kulisek; p. 182 b: reisegraf.ch; pp. 182–183 bi: Barbora Martinakova; p. 183 b: Pi-Lens; p. 184 b: Pecold; pp. 184–185 bi: Emi330; p. 185 m: sixtyeightwest; p. 185 b: Roger Asbury; p. 186 m: Mady MacDonald; pp. 186–187 bi: oksana. perkins; p. 187 t: Mady MacDonald; pp. 188–189 bi: Serge Skiba; p. 189 b: Tara Kenny; p. 190 b: Rainer Lesniewski; pp. 190–191 bi: Dancestrokes; p. 192: Manuel Lacoste; p. 193: RUBEN M RAMOS; pp. 194–195 bi: Danita Delmont; p. 195 t: SARIN KUNTHONG; p. 196 t: Danita Delmont; pp. 196–197 bi: GROGL; p. 198 t: Spiroview Inc; p. 198 m: Sergey Uryadnikov; p. 198 b: Alexandr Vlassyuk; p. 199 t: corlaffra; p. 199 m: AndreAnita; p. 199 b: Pi-Lens; p. 200 t: Eric Isselee; p. 200 m: Pi-Lens; p. 200 b: A Cotton Photo; p. 201 t: Cindy Creighton; p. 201 m: Andrew Sutton; p. 201 b: Randy Bjorklund; p. 202 t: Fabien Monteil; p. 202 bl: Natalya Osipova; p. 202 br: aleksander hunta; pp. 202–203 bi: Phutcharapan Mdr; p. 203 tl: RLS Photo; p. 203 tr: The Old Major; p. 203 bl: Samantha H; p. 203 br: Matt Jeppson; p. 204 t: Sanne vd Berg Fotografie; p. 205 tl: Dora Zett; p. 205 r: cynoclub; p. 205 b: Nancy Bauer; p. 206 t: Tom Middleton; pp. 206–207 bi: Kevin Xu Photography; p. 207 tl: Wolfgang Kruck; p. 207 tr: FloridaStock; p. 207 m: Kent Ellington; p. 208 t: Eileen Kumpf; p. 208 ml: Mironmax Studio; p. 208 mr: Paul Reeves Photography; p. 208 b: Bob Silverman CDN; pp. 208–209 bi: JHVEPhoto; p. 210 b: Howard Sandler; pp. 210–211 bi: BGSmith; p. 212 b : David P. Lewis; pp. 212–213 bi: Ronnie Chua; p. 213 b: karenfoleyphotography; p. 214: cvrestan; p. 215 t: Krishna.Wu; p. 215 bl: marevos imaging; p. 215 br: Russ Heinl; p. 216 t: Shawna and Damien Richard; p. 216 b: Elena11; p. 217 b: Lopolo; p. 218 t: Rainer Lesniewski; p.

218 m: Artifan; p. 218 b: Andrew Park; pp. 218–219 bi: best_vector; p. 219 t: bonecar1216; p. 219 m: Kin Fok; p. 219 b: Gary Goldberg; p. 220 t: Weekend Warrior Photos; p. 220 bl: Ray Yang; p. 220 br: puttsk; p. 221 t: Jana Kasparova; p. 221 b: Ferenc Cegledi; p. 222 tl: SurangaSL; p. 222 tr: Tyler Olson; p. 222 b: RUBEN M RAMOS; p. 223 bl: Rainer Lesniewski; p. 223 br: Sublimage; p. 224 t: eskystudio; p. 224 b: jlazouphoto; p. 225: 2009fotofriends; pp. 226–227: DedMityay; pp. 228–229: Taiga; pp. 230–231: Blaze986; pp. 232–233: Elena Elisseeva; pp. 234–235: Andriy Blokhin; pp. 236–237: 2009fotofriends; pp. 238–239: Mikhail Zapolskyi; p. 240 br: Everett Historical; pp. 240–241 bi: greenmax; p. 241 b: Nattakorn_Maneerat; pp. 242–243 bi: best_vector; pp. 244–245 bi: vmargineanu; p. 245 bl: rhfletcher; p. 245 br: Emylia; p. 246 t: Lana Langlois; p. 246 mr: Matt Benoit; p. 246 bl: Elena Elisseeva; p. 246 br: Keith Homan; pp. 246–247 bi: CobraCZ; p. 247 bl: worrachet sansing; p. 247 br: Joshua Resnick; pp. 248–249 bi: Ollyy; p. 249 t: Craig Russell; p. 249 b: Chereliss; p. 250: jdross75; p. 251 t: Sean Pavone; p. 251 b: catwalker; p. 252 t: neftali; p. 252 b: Kathy Hutchins; p. 253 t: Tinseltown; p. 253 ml: catwalker; p. 253 mc: Kathy Hutchins; p. 254 l: Kathy Hutchins; p. 254 r: lev radin; p. 255 l: lev radin; p. 255 c: Tinseltown; p. 255 r: s_bukley; p. 256 b: Glynnis Jones; pp. 256–257 bi: LoopAll; p. 257 t: Featureflash Photo Agency; p. 257 b: Featureflash; p. 258 t: Tero Vesalainen; p. 258 m: s_bukley; p. 258 bl: DFree; p. 258 br: Jaguar PS; p. 259 t: Tinseltown; pp. 260–261 bi: Igor Bulgarin; p. 261 tl: VGstockstudio; p. 261 tr: Igor Bulgarin; p. 262 t: Gilberto Mesquita; p. 262 m: EQRoy; p. 262 b: mikecphoto; pp. 262–263 bi: meunierd; p. 264 t: Tony Moran; p. 264 bl: Keith Homan; p. 265 t: Alexander Tolstykh; p. 266 l: Larich; p. 266 r: DFree; pp. 266–267 bi: jeremykramerdesign; p. 267 t: Kathy Hutchins; p. 267 m: fyv6561; p. 267 b: Bobnevv; pp. 270–271 bi: mariakray; pp. 272–273 bi: best_vector; p. 273 t: klarka0608; p. 275 t: Iurii Osadchi; p. 275 b: Iurii Osadchi; p. 276 l: Michele Morrone; p. 276 r: Everett Collection; p. 277 tr: Debby Wong; p. 277 b: Art Babych; p. 278 b: Photo Works; pp. 278–279 bi: David Lee; p. 281 b: Olga Besnard; p. 282 b: Stefan Holm; pp. 282–283 bi: Frame Art; p. 284 bl: Mikolaj Barbanell; pp. 284–285 bi: robin.ph; pp. 286–287 bi: BlueButterfly; p. 288 b: simontop; p. 289 t: Yurgentum; p. 289 m: bearink; p. 289 b: Gavin Napier; p. 292 t: Rena Schild; p. 292 m: lev radin; p. 292 b: mooinblack; p. 293 t: Chris McPhee; p. 294 tl: Louis.Roth; p. 294 tr: Shawn Goldberg; p. 294 b: Marc Bruxelle; p. 295 t: Canadapanda; p. 295 m: Maridav;

Canada Post
p. 48 tr: Canada Post Corporation, 2000; p. 75 tr: Canada Post Corporation, 1933; p. 77 t: Canada Post Corporation, 1983; p. 82 tr: Canada Post Corporation, 1980; p. 86 bl: Canada Post Corporation, 1934; p. 87 mr: Canada Post Corporation, 2004; p. 84: Canada Post Corporation, 1981; p. 96 l: Canada Post Corporation, 1998; p. 129 t: Canada Post Corporation, 1998; p. 130 m: Canada Post Corporation, 1973; p. 196 b: Canada Post Corporation, 1970; p. 204 b: Canada Post Corporation, 1988

Canadian Paralympic Committee
p. 286 t: Canadian Paralympic Committee; p. 286 b: Canadian Paralympic Committee; p. 287 t: Canadian Paralympic Committee; p. 287 m: Canadian Paralympic Committee; p. 287 b: Canadian Paralympic Committee

Canadian Space Agency
p. 57 tr: Canadian Space Agency; p. 57 bl: Canadian Space Agency; p. 127 b: SpaceX

Dominion Diamond Mines
p. 188 t: Dominion Diamond Mines; p. 189 t: Dominion Diamond Mines

Dreamstime
p. 264 b: Daicokuebisu/Dreamstime.com; p. 272 t: Jerry Coli/Dreamstime.com; p. 279 t: Jerry Coli/Dreamstime.com; p. 279 b: Jerry Coli/Dreamstime.com; p. 308 b: Manuel Machado/Dreamstime.com

Hockey Hall of Fame
p. 271 t: Graphic Artists/Hockey Hall of Fame; p. 271 m: James Rice/Hockey Hall of Fame; p. 274 m: James Welch/Hockey Hall of Fame; p. 274 b: Matthew Manor/Hockey Hall of Fame

Hudson's Bay Comapny Archive
p. 88 l: HBCA 1987/363-C-211/2 "Hudson's Bay Company Store, Calgary 1884"

iStock
p. 51 tr: alicat; p. 53 br: Lokibaho

Library and Archives Canada
p. 43 br: Charles A. Aylett/Library and Archives Canada/C-014090; p. 60 tl: Arthur S. Goss/Library and Archives Canada/ PA-123481; p. 73 m: Library and Archives Canada/PA-202182; p. 76: Library and Archives Canada/NMC24974; p. 92 b: Library and Archives Canada, Acc. No. 1938-211-1; p. 92 tr: L'abbé Joseph Chabert, Libabry and Archives Canada, Acc. No. 1982-188-1; p. 93: Canada. Dept. of National Defence/Library and Archives Canada/ PA-001017; p. 95 l: Library and Archives Canada, Acc. No. 1977-64-12; p. 95 r: Arthur Roy/Library and Archives Canada / PA-046989; p. 97 r: Library and Archives Canada, Acc. No. 1994-272-1; p. 102 t: Library and Archives Canada/C-005327; p. 102 b: William James Topley/Library and Archives Canada/ C-000697; p. 103 t: William James Topley/ Library and Archives Canada/C-068645; p. 103 m: William James Topley/Library and Archives Canada/PA-027222; p. 104 t: William James Topley/Library and Archives Canada/C-001971; p. 105 b: Library and Archives Canada/C-10461; p. 105 m: Library and Archives Canada/C-000687; p. 106 t: Gar Lunney/Library and Archives Canada/ C-006779; p. 106 m: Duncan Cameron/ Library and Archives Canada/e007150485; p. 107 t: Arnaud Maggs/Library and Arcives Canada/R7959-6337; p. 107 m: Library and Archives Canada; p. 147 t: Library and Archives Canada/PA-800076; p. 179 t: Canada. Patent and Copyright Office/Library and Archives Canada/PA-029915; p. 187 b: Library and Archives Canada/PA-013422; p. 240 bl: Library and Archives Canada/PA 116389; p. 243 b: A. Bazinet/Library and Archives Canada/C-003286; p. 281 m: Library and Archives Canada/National Film Board fonds/e010966709; p. 284 t: E. Ferrat/National Film Board of Canada. Photothèque/Library and Archives Canada

Library of Congress Archives
p. 103 b: Library of Congress Archives: LC-DIG-ggbain-16896; p. 105 t: Library of Congress Archives: LC-USW33-019079-D; p. 291 t: Library of Congress Archives: LC-DIG-ggbain-00145; p. 257 m: Library of Congress Archives: LC-USZ62-101394

Manitoba Sports Hall of Fame
p. 282 t: Manitoba Sports Hall of Fame & Museum Inc

NASA
p. 41 t: NASA images; p. 43 tl: NASA images; p. 43 ml: NASA images; p. 55 t: NASA images; p. 217 t: NASA Earth Observatory image by Joshua Stevens; p. 223 t: Nasa WorldWind

Reuters
p. 55 b: Reuters/J.P. Moczulski; p. 274 t: Reuters/Andrew Wallace ANW; p. 278 t: Reuters/Jim Young

Revelstoke Museum and Archives
p. 242 b: Revelstoke Museum and Archives/ Joseph Daem collection

Scholastic Canada
p. 265 b: Scholastic Canada

The Canadian Press
p. 64: The Globe and Mail/Tibor Kolley

INDEX

Page numbers in bolded italics refer to text with illustrations.